The Way of the Peaceful Woman

Awaken the Power of You, Create a Life You Love,

and Set Yourself Free

By

Amy Beth Acker, LCSW

A Gift For You

The Way of the Peaceful Woman is a blueprint for finding the peace already available inside you and is full of tools to empower you to change your thoughts, feelings, actions, and beliefs in order to awaken the power of you, create a life you love, and free yourself of anything that holds you back from being the highest version of yourself.

I created a bonus section for my book called *Peaceful Body* and it is a full-length e-book designed to teach you how to work in harmony with your body's natural rhythms and tap into the transformative power of your feminine energy.

Together, *The Way of the Peaceful Woman* and *Peaceful Body* will provide you with a holistic, whole-person guide to help you find lasting balance and wellness in your life.

Please visit amybethacker.com/bonus to claim your free ebook, *Peaceful Body*.

Enjoy!

~Amy

The Way of the Peaceful Woman

Awaken the Power of You, Create a Life You Love, and Set Yourself Free

By Amy Beth Acker, LCSW

Clarity Books

150 West End Ave

Somerville, NJ 08876

(973) 769-2401

Email: Amy@AmyBethAcker.com

Website: AmyBethAcker.com

ISBN: 978-0-578-49136-3

Cover design: Amanda Raynor Hayes

Interior design: Manuel Garfo

This book is dedicated to the women who came before me.

Especially Ellen, Florence, and Bella.

And for the women who have come after me.

Especially Violet and Emily.

Table of Contents

"Ours is not the task of fixing the entire world at once, but of stretching out to mend the part of the world that is within our reach."
—*Clarissa Pinkola Estés*

"We think that the point is to pass the test or overcome the problem, but the truth is that things don't really get solved. They come together and they fall apart. Then they come together again and fall apart again. It's just like that. The healing comes from letting there be room for all of this to happen: room for grief, for relief, for misery, for joy."
—*Pema Chödrön*

"Ego says, 'Once everything falls into place, I'll feel peace.' Spirit says, 'Find your peace, then everything will fall into place.'"
—*Marianne Williamson*

Part 1: In Search of Peace

Who You Are

This book is for every woman who feels stressed, burnt-out, frustrated, and/or stuck. It's for every woman who puts the comfort of others, even strangers, before her own.

If you're reading this book, you've likely experienced a crisis in your life. In fact, you may even be living one right now. Maybe it's a test result that served as a wake-up call. Maybe it's a crucial ball dropped at the worst possible time (like forgetting to pick up a child or blanking on a major deadline at work), or maybe it's just a quiet voice that has grown increasingly insistent that things simply cannot go on this way.

These crises are life's way of opening our eyes to what is no longer working for us in our lives. They are blessings in disguise alerting us to the fact that our priorities have gone off kilter. They help us to recognize that the physical, emotional or spiritual abuse we are inflicting on ourselves must change and it must change now.

As women, we are trained from an early age to not burden others with who we are. We are taught that if we are true to ourselves, we will harm others. Taking time for yourself means the people you love most will lose out. Speaking your truth means someone else will be disappointed. Most of us live our lives believing that it is impossible to be authentic and to live with personal integrity without alienating or hurting everyone around us.

That stops today.

This book is designed to help you move out of crisis and into peace. It will give you both concrete tools and new ways of thinking that will help you to recognize yourself for who you really are: powerful and whole with everything you need to create a life you love already inside you.

It is designed to help you prioritize your own needs, to get reacquainted with yourself, and to become the most authentic, peaceful, and joyful version of you. This book is a practice in renewal: literally the act of making yourself new again, repairing what is broken or no longer working, and starting over with fresh eyes and a fresh heart.

I honor you for opening your heart to what this book has to offer. It takes courage to believe that positive change is possible. Whatever happened in the past has been leading to this moment, and I'm glad you're here as we begin our journey together.

The Burden of Burnout

Most of us have lives that are full of big things like relationships, careers, family and friend commitments, and managing our own health and happiness. They're also full of the little things like news feeds, buying birthday presents, shopping for new pants, clipping our toenails, and remembering to put the laundry in the dryer. The big and small things all take up space in our minds and our lives either because we believe they will make us happier or because we are told we "have to" do them or some combination of both.

Most of us have worked hard to attain the things in life that we hold closest to our hearts and we want nothing more than to appreciate them to the fullest. Unfortunately, this becomes difficult when we're stressed, burnt-out, or just plain overwhelmed with the amount of time and energy it takes to keep up with all the moving parts in our lives.

When we try to be great at everything and be everything to everyone, life can start to feel much more like a juggling act with one too many balls in the air, and much less like the joyful journey we envisioned when we pursued these things in the first place.

We feel pride and satisfaction with our lives when we allow ourselves to focus on our achievements and successes (or when we can at least get it to look good from the outside), and we feel overwhelmed, stressed, and frazzled when we get caught up in the day-to-day frenzy of what needs to be done and how much there still is to do.

The truth is we cannot operate at our best in any area of life when we are worn down, from being chronically "busy". Yet still, we try to convince ourselves that things will be better if we can just get through this difficult day, this hectic week or this crazy year. We convince ourselves that peace is somewhere just over the horizon when we finally get a promotion or change careers or find a partner or when our kids are out of diapers or preschool or out of college. Meanwhile, we're so busy chasing happiness, we miss out on our lives—especially the good stuff like connecting with the people we love, being attuned to our deepest selves, creative expression, and the feeling of pure, effortless fun.

This book is about learning a new way of approaching the world. It's about living with intention and living from your soul. It's about connecting with your deepest desires and fully owning them. It's about prioritizing yourself not only for yourself but to add to the greater collective good. It's about giving the world, and more importantly, yourself a gift: the gift of you at your most authentic.

In other words, this book is about finding peace no matter what.

We can't give to others what we don't have for ourselves. When we embody the energy and emotions we wish to have reflected back to us, we increase the love, joy, and connection for everyone. More importantly, we become able to give ourselves in each moment what has previously seemed always just out of reach: a life that is in alignment with who we are at a soul-level.

How to Use This Book

If you don't already have a journal, you should purchase one before diving in. It doesn't have to be fancy, though it certainly can be if that appeals to you. For our purposes, a marble notebook from the dollar store will work just as well as an engraved leather one.

Although this book is full of strategies for greater peace that can be used immediately, it's not intended to make you even more overwhelmed by suggesting you apply everything you read to your life right away.

At the end of each section of this book, you will find journal questions to help you integrate and process the information you just read. These questions will help you to more deeply understand the material and to apply it to your own unique situation. Take your time with these questions and use them to discover more about who you are: past, present and future.

Peace is always about expansion and being open to receive whatever gifts life has for you in any particular moment. Therefore, it should not feel like one more task to check off on your to do list. Adding more stress and obligation is never the path to peace and the best approach to bringing peace into your life is the one that works best for you.

The peaceful woman's way is all about connection: to your intuition, your highest self, and your deepest desires. This book is designed to help you make meaningful, lasting positive changes in the areas of your life where you feel you need it most. I invite you to honor your desire to live a life you truly love and let that desire be your guide as you read this book and do its exercises.

Remember that our brains are wired to avoid change. Staying with what feels safe and familiar is how humans have survived the past few million years. Doing something different is probably going to feel scary and uncomfortable but our personal evolution requires us to step outside our comfort zones with open hearts and open minds.

I encourage you to approach this book with openness, curiosity, and intention. If, however, you lose sight of your work here for a period of time, give yourself grace. Notice that you've gotten away from that intention, be honest and gentle with yourself about what has gotten in the way, and come back here where you left off. Like an old friend, it will always be there for you when you're ready.

Use any setbacks that come up as a reminder to take some time to check in and explore whether your resistance is because you are going too fast and you need some time to catch up with your evolving brain, or whether it's because something has gotten out of alignment and you need to go deeper into the work.

Before You Get Started

Before you dive in, I invite you to take a few moments with your journal and write down your intentions for reading *The Way of The Peaceful Woman*. There is probably something that drew you to this book and led you to believe that it would support you in whatever area of your life you're looking for support in.

For example, maybe you find yourself snapping at your partner or kids when they do something that gets under your skin—and it seems like they're always doing something to get under your skin. Or maybe you're stressed at work, and you've been waking up in the middle of the night worrying about how you're going to tackle your mile-long to-do list the next day. Or maybe you've been meaning to do something for yourself for once, but you feel like you already don't do all the things you "should" be doing for everyone else. Maybe you just know something is off but you aren't sure how to make it better because you aren't sure what the problem really is.

This book can help you gain control over unnecessary suffering in your life. It is here to support you in cultivating awareness and greater presence, and learning to find peace in each moment, regardless of the external circumstances. Trust that this is possible for you even if right now it's hard to imagine what it will look like.

When we awaken our feminine power, we become conscious stewards of the energy by which everything lives. We cultivate a relationship to ourselves that allows the voices of perfectionism and people-pleasing to be quieted so that we can show up in the world as the whole, perfect, and complete women we already are.

The Way of the Peaceful Woman is not about creating a life that looks good on paper or that looks like success to others. It's much more than an attempt at preventing burnout or trying to lessen the tidal wave of panic if you're already well past the burnout stage. It's about honoring the highest version of yourself by working with the flow of your own creativity, intuition, and inner-wisdom.

It's important to note that without self-love and self-compassion, there is no way to be with peace. The path to peace is about putting the highest priority in honoring and expressing our truest, most authentic selves, practicing self-love and connection with our own creative energy and inner-wisdom, and being fully present in the moment, regardless of our external circumstances.

I believe our suffering is not only done to us, it's also done within us. The question then becomes not how can I connect to the experience of peace inside me, but what am I doing to block it in this moment and how can I start to see suffering as a friend and a teacher?

This book will help you to answer that question.

- My intentions for reading this book are for me to be comfortable with my Authentic self, and allow her to flourish.
- My other intentions are to reunite with peace, self compassion and my highest self. To live a more mindful and conscious life.

An Important Message

If you notice as you read this book that feelings are coming up that are too difficult to process or deal with on your own, such as unresolved trauma, grief, severe anxiety or depression, you should take a break and seek out the help of a good therapist.

Though my profession is a psychotherapist, this book is not psychotherapy or counseling and does not substitute in any way for individual mental health treatment.

Therapy can be a powerful tool on your journey. It has the power to give meaning to your past so it becomes wisdom, to give clarity to your future so it can be lived with intention, and to help you experience peace in the present moment.

If you are already under the care of a counselor or therapist, be sure to discuss what you are learning and working on in this book so that they can help you process and customize the experience even further to fit your personal needs.

The point of this journey isn't to reach any particular destination, it's about creating a practice that allows us to be fully awake each moment of our lives.

Thank you for joining me. Let's get started.

Getting Clear

Here are some questions to consider to help get you started with intention on your journey:

- What drew you to this book?

- What do you hope will be different in your life experience by the time you've finished it?

- What obstacles or challenges do you anticipate will present themselves as you pursue growth and positive change? (Not enough time? Competing priorities? Uncertainty about the value?)

- What core strengths do you already have within you that will help you make your intentions for this book a reality?

- How did you define peace before reading this section? What thoughts do you have about peace after reading it?

- What messages have you received from family or mentors about what it looks and feels like to experience peace in your daily life? If you don't recall receiving any direct messages, what does this tell you?

- What are the greatest blocks to peace in your life right now? Are they different now than in the past? What would have to change in order for peace to be possible in these areas?

- Describe an area of your life where you have felt or currently feel peace. What makes it possible? How is it different than the other areas of your life?

- What would your life look like if peace were accessible to you at any moment no matter what the circumstances? How would you spend your time? How would your relationships with others and with yourself change?

Part 2: Awaken the Power of You

Letting Go of Perfect

Serena, a 38-year-old wife, mother, and corporate brand strategist felt like she was in over her head. She was working long hours that included frequent travel in her job at a startup, racing home to take care of her 18-month-old and 4-year-old before they went to bed, spending time with her dad, who was depressed after the death of her mother, and trying to figure out a way to connect with her husband, Kevin. Unfortunately, lately, most of Serena's conversations with Kevin took place through text and their limited time together consisted of doing work next to each other in bed before passing out.

Serena was so overwhelmed that she had gotten to a point where she no longer felt she could get through a day without several strong coffees in the morning and a regular supply of energy drinks throughout the rest of the day. She often finished the last one right before she went to bed after working late into the night. She frequently experienced headaches, hadn't gotten a haircut in over a year, and had recently had her first panic attack while in the middle of a marketing presentation on a business trip.

Despite her mind and body's strong signals that it was time to make changes in her life, Serena had convinced herself that change wasn't possible. She believed that although her stress levels were high and she wasn't enjoying her life very much, there was no way to make things better. She instead justified her hectic lifestyle by telling herself that the situation was only temporary and would at some point improve on its own.

"As soon as the kids are older…" "As soon as my company is able to hire more support…" "As soon as my dad is feeling better…I'll have more time and things will be easier."

The wake-up call came when she passed out from exhaustion while manning a table at an event ironically geared toward professional women and work/life balance.

When I saw Serena for our first counseling session, she told me through anxious tears, "It feels like I'm climbing up a mountain with a boulder strapped to my back. I try to take a step forward but I just get dragged down to the beginning with the weight of it all."

"What would feel like relief in this moment?" I asked her.

It was a question she had never contemplated before. She told me that relief would feel like having less on her plate, fewer people depending on her, and more time for herself. However, she said, those things were all impossible, given that she both wanted and needed to work and both wanted and needed her family.

We agreed to work together to devise a plan to stop adding obligations to her life and instead get clear on what she truly valued. We would then work together to subtract anything that didn't align with those values.

Serena's plan included stepping down from several non-mandatory obligations at work that she had taken on because "no one else can has time to do it," saying "no" to any further requests of her time, outsourcing all non-essential tasks at home so she could spend her time relaxing and enjoying her family, and enlisting the help of her brother to help her support their father.

Our clinical work included cognitive-behavioral therapy (a form of therapy that helps the client to question and challenge negative thoughts and beliefs),[1] mindfulness training[2] such as deep breathing and muscle relaxation, and doing the deeper work of examining what

---

[1] One of many, many studies demonstrating the effectiveness of CBT for anxiety: Linden, M., D. Zubraegel, T. Baer, U. Franke, P. Schlattmann. 2005. Efficacy of Cognitive behavioral therapy in generalized anxiety disorders. Results of a controlled clinical trial (Berlin CBT-GAD study). *Psychotherapy and Psychosomatics.* https://doi.org/10.1371/journal.pone.0061713

[2] An overview of just some of the research supporting the efficacy of using mindfulness in therapy: Davis, D., and J. Hayes. 2011. What are the benefits of mindfulness? A practice review of psychotherapy-related research. *Psychotherapy.* Vol. 48, No. 2, 198–208

was behind her punishing, unforgiving goals and self-imposed desire to please and achieve. I also worked to help Serena redefine success on her own terms, not by what her friends, parents, or society thought was best for her.

Serena looked at the messages she received as a child: to value effort and hard work regardless of personal cost, a mindset based on scarcity and competition, and a deep-seated belief that no matter what she did, she was never good enough. She slowly came to the realization that these beliefs were no longer in alignment with what she wanted for her life. She also came to understand that her body was giving her an important message that day she fainted: that forcing more onto her plate in desperate pursuit of metaphorical gold stars was destroying her ability to have the very things she wanted most in life.

As Serena began to identify her new values of creative self-expression, generosity to self and others, plenty of room for margin in her days, and regular fun for its own sake, she quickly realized that none of those values could be fully embodied without first changing her relationship with herself. She needed to let go of the person she had always thought she was supposed to be in order to honor the person she was.

This was no simple task, given that doing it required her to let go of a worldview she had built her entire life around yet was no longer working for her. Yet little by little, Serena was able to design a new life for herself, built on a foundation of new thinking.

Serena was finally able to let go of the idea that she had to be and do everything for everyone in order to have value and be a success. Instead, she embraced the notion that the only way to have value was to value herself and the only way to experience success was to have a successful present moment. It was still a very full life, now but with plenty of room to breathe, and now full of the right things in the right amounts for her.

Your Stressed-Out Nervous System

Part of understanding the path to peace involves understanding the effect stress has on us physically. Let's take a quick look at the science behind this.

Your nervous system is a system in your body that includes your brain, spinal cord, nerves, and sense organs. It receives, interprets, and responds to stimuli both in your body and in the environment around you. Your nervous system works together with your endocrine system—the system that produces, dispenses, and regulates hormones—to allow you to physically, intellectually, and emotionally experience and interact with the world.[3]

The autonomic nervous system is the division of your nervous system that works unconsciously. In other words, it is responsible for all the processes that keep you alive but that you don't have to think

---

[3] This PDF e-book has great, detailed information about what the autonomic system is and how it works: Goldstein, D. 2016. *Principles of Autonomic Medicine* (PDF) (free online version ed.). Bethesda, Maryland: National Institute of Neurological Disorders and Stroke, National Institutes of Health.

about in order to make them work. It works in two modes: sympathetic and parasympathetic.

The sympathetic nervous system is our fight, flight, or freeze response. It works together with the endocrine system to dispense chemicals and hormones such as cortisol, adrenaline, and norepinephrine when we need to respond to a threat. These chemicals cause physical changes in our bodies such as dilated pupils (to focus without distraction on the threat), increased heart rate and respiration (to increase blood flow and oxygen to our muscles and tissues), and tensed muscles (to decrease reaction times). Flipping to survival mode, it also affects how we process information in our brains as solving the problem of how to survive becomes the primary function.[4]

The sympathetic nervous system is what keeps us alive during life or death situations and helps us to discern if there is danger in our environment that we need to react to. This mechanism is what has kept our ancestors alive for millions of years.

In modern times, our sympathetic nervous system is still very much an integral part of our daily existence. However, since we are rarely in life

---

[4] Another great, detailed description of how the autonomic nervous system works: McCorry LK. Physiology of the autonomic nervous system. *Am J Pharm Educ*. 2007;71(4):78.

or death situations, the sympathetic nervous system now focuses on other sources of stress and reacts to them with the exact same physical and cognitive responses our ancestors experienced when they were being chased by bears or going to war with a neighboring tribe.[5]

Our brains are designed to use the sympathetic nervous system to find and attempt to solve problems in order to keep us alive. Unfortunately, as we have evolved, we have gotten so good at focusing on the problems in our lives and in the world, that it has become as automatic and unconscious as breathing. Of course, this takes a serious physical, emotional, and spiritual toll on us in ways we'll explore a little further on.

The parasympathetic nervous system is responsible for our "rest and digest" and "feed and breed" activities—basically the processes we undertake when our bodies are in a relaxed state and able to focus on things outside our immediate survival.[6] When our nervous systems are in the parasympathetic mode, we feel calm and relaxed and our brains are able to make conscious intentional decisions.

Being in the parasympathetic nervous system allows us to think creatively and abstractly and to connect with our inner-wisdom and intu-

---

[5] For more about what the stress response is and how it works: Harvard Health Publishing. 2018. Understanding the Stress Response: Chronic Activation of this Survival Mechanism Impairs Health. https://www.health.harvard.edu/staying-healthy/understanding-the-stress-response

[6] McCorry LK. Physiology of the autonomic nervous system. *Am J Pharm Educ.* 2007;71(4):78.

ition. It enables us to take thoughtful, considered action, taking into account what we have learned from our past, what we desire from the future, and who we are in the present moment.[7] In other words, we are able to be in integrity with our highest, most authentic selves.

Both the sympathetic and parasympathetic nervous systems are indispensable to living our lives. Our sympathetic nervous system keeps us safe and out of harm's way while our parasympathetic nervous system allows us to give our lives meaning, be present and live with purpose.

The problem comes when we experience trauma or chronic stress and our sympathetic (threat response) system takes over, causing us to live in the past where the terrible thing happened or in the future where we fear they will happen again. Because neither the past nor the future currently exists (except in our thoughts), we lose our present selves and we become small, scared, and confused about who we really are and what we really want out of life. We lose purpose and meaning and consequently lose our quality of life. This is called sympathetic dominance.[8]

---

[7] From the course I took through PESI to become a Clinical Trauma Professional: Gentry, E., R. Rhoton. 2017. *Certified Clinical Trauma Professional Intensive Training Course.* Module 1: The History and Evolution of Traumatic Stress, Grief, and Loss.

[8] Gentry, E., R. Rhoton. (2017). *Certified Clinical Trauma Professional Intensive Training Course.* Module 1: The History and Evolution of Traumatic Stress, Grief, and Loss.

To be clear, when I refer to experiencing trauma, which leads to sympathetic dominance, I don't necessarily mean one specific, tragic event like a car crash or a sexual assault, though those events obviously qualify as traumatic. I am also referring to chronic, low-intensity activators such as growing up in a chaotic, aggressive, or shaming environment, experiencing financial or familial instability as a child or adult, or even just chronic job, relationship or general life stress. Sympathetic dominance can be the product of any situation that causes a repeated perception of threat and produces small doses of fight or flight responses over a period of time.

When we're operating in our sympathetic nervous system chronically, our brains become impulsive, irrational, illogical, and have little capacity for self-evaluation or self-reflection. We lose our ability to self-regulate our thoughts, emotions, or actions. We become unable to establish goals and take action to obtain them. We may feel angry, restless, anxious, irritable, hostile, unfocused, defensive, numb, distracted, stuck, overwhelmed, or just sad.[9] Any time you snap at a co-worker, yell at your kids or become unable to stop replaying an awkward interaction you had five days ago in your head, you're in sympathetic dominance.

---

[9] A look at how chronic stress can change the wiring of the brain and the ways the brain can rewire itself over time due to its plastic nature: McEwen, BS. (2017). Neurobiological and systemic effects of chronic stress. *Chronic Stress (Thousand Oaks)*.doi: 10.1177/2470547017692328. Epub 2017 Apr 10.

Ultimately, sympathetic dominance leads us to make snap judgments and react before we've given ourselves a chance to fully process the information. Our memories become less and less reliable and our present experience gets contaminated by an unprocessed past.[10] Logic and reasoning take a back seat, and it becomes increasingly difficult to behave in ways that support a positive self-image and worldview. When we are in sympathetic dominance, we are also much more likely engage in mental "buffering," which is any behavior such as binge TV watching, social media scrolling, over-drinking, or overeating designed to distract us from our uncomfortable emotions.

If any of the above describes you, be aware that these behaviors shouldn't be labeled as "bad" or "wrong," but rather as evidence that your sympathetic nervous system is currently (and possibly chronically) in use. Your brain is working exactly as it's supposed to—it was designed to be adaptive, and if you're in chronic stress, it will want to protect you by responding to anything it determines to be a threat as quickly and efficiently as possible.[11] The more your sympathetic nervous system gets activated in your daily life, the stronger it's pathways in your brain get.

---

[10] An in-depth look at the biology behind this: McEwen, BS, R.M. Sapolosky. 1995. Stress and cognitive function. *Current Opinion in Neurobiology*. Apr. 5(2):205-16.

[11] More research on how the brain adopts maladaptive behaviors in response to chronic stress: Huether, G., S. Doering, U. Rüger, E. Rüger, G. Schüssler. 1999 The stress reaction process and the adaptive modification and reorganization of neuronal networks. *Psychiatry Research Journal* Jul 30;87(1):83-95.

However, simply having awareness of the inner-workings of your brain can empower you to become aware or your automatic responses, get clear on what no longer serves you, and take steps toward peace.

This is Your Brain on Stress

B eing in a constant state of sympathetic dominance (stress) can affect every area of our lives. We can recognize it easily if we know the emotions to look for. Some symptoms of chronic stress include feeling:

- Stuck or blocked

- Frustrated with others, situations, or your life in general

- Frazzled, crazed, anxious, fearful or panicked

- Chronically sick or unhealthy

- Unfulfilled

- Alone, shamed, closed off

- Rageful, resentful

- Victimized, suffocated[12]

Our emotions are our first-line warning system that something is not right. They are a powerful tool for letting us know when we have got-

---

[12] A phenomenal book on the feminine archetype: Pinkola Estés, C. 1992. *Women Who Run With the Wolves: Myths and Stories of the Wild Woman Archetype*. New York: Random House.

ten out of alignment. When we don't listen to our warning bells, sympathetic dominance might translate into:

- Creating strict rules about what "success" and "failure" look like in life
- Ignoring physical and emotional boundaries (your own or others') in service of accomplishing goals
- Never starting a new project due to feeling overwhelmed or uninspired
- Starting many projects and never finishing any of them
- An identity that relies on achievements
- Hustling to make a goal happen regardless of cost
- Being guided by impulse instead of values
- Allowing physical and psychological well-being to constantly come in last place after all other priorities
- Making decisions or spending money out of fear
- Feeling disconnected from the people and things you love and care about most
- Relating to others from a place of defensiveness or judgment

If you can identify yourself in these descriptions, know that you are not alone. These are universal stories I hear over and over again from women who come to therapy. I know how terrible it can feel to live them because I have at one time or another lived them all myself. It is a devastating moment when you realize you've become a person you don't like to be. And yet, that is the moment when it becomes possible to start moving toward a life that reflects your true self.

It's possible for all of us to have freedom from the state of sympathetic dominance that robs us of our peace. In fact, unlike other things we want in life, it's not something we have to achieve or go out and make happen. Connecting to peace is about connecting to the energy of the divine already inside each of us. Peace is our most natural state. We don't need to create it, only to remove what's blocking us from experiencing what's already there.

When we are acting with intention and attunement to our hearts and the deeper world around us, we are in the parasympathetic nervous system. Remember that the parasympathetic nervous system is activated when our minds and bodies are able to be in a sustained relaxed state. (Note: this doesn't necessarily mean deep meditation or sleep, but rather, approaching life with presence, openness, and willingness to be with whatever shows up in the moment.) Therefore, our feelings are the first and most accessible signs that we are operating in our parasympathetic nervous systems. We feel:

- Sovereign, balanced

- Confident, knowing, patient

- Open, receptive, expansive

- Fulfilled, peaceful, rested

- Connected, tuned-in, guided, living with integrity

- Joyful, fun-filled, light-hearted, warm

- Creative, inspired, intentional

- Wholehearted

- Kind, loving, gentle, ease-full, flowing

These feelings might translate into experiences in your life such as:

- Attracting what you want to you instead of struggling to make it happen

- Leaving yourself open to different possibilities and ways of moving forward toward a desired outcome

- Creating community and collaboration with like-minded people

- Not being afraid to ask for and expect support all the time, not just when there's no choice or things have gotten out of hand

- Taking good care of yourself, in the ways that feel good and right for you

- Honoring and embracing your limitations

- Putting your energy and attention toward relationships where you find the greatest value and enjoyment
- Focusing on the journey, not the end result, and feeling confident and relaxed along the way
- Seeing the big picture as well as the beauty in the details
- Staying open to what life has to offer
- Being guided by your inner-wisdom and creativity to solve problems
- Valuing rest and renewal as crucial aspects of a rich, fulfilling life
- Having fun on a regular basis
- Staying conscious of and gently enforcing your boundaries
- Speaking your truth in ways that others can hear it
- Having more than enough time, energy, and support in your daily life

Ultimately, these experiences cannot happen when we are in sympathetic dominance. Chronic stress and sympathetic dominance can severely impact the way our brains process information, the way we regulate ourselves, and our ability to be in tune with others and in alignment with our values.

Understanding how our brains work gives us a context and a framework to make positive changes in our lives. It also helps to normalize feelings and experiences that can feel both terrible and unique to us.

There are a range of human emotions and we all experience all of them at one time or another because we're all human. We are all doing the best we can and we all would like to be the best version of ourselves all the time. When we act or react in ways that don't feel good for us, it helps to know it is not a symptom of some deep character flaw, but rather a sign of strength. Our "negative" thoughts, feelings, and behaviors are the ways our brains have helped us survive in our lives. If those ways are no longer working for us, the beauty of awareness and free-will is that we can always choose something different.

Sometimes that's easier to do than others, but knowledge is power and change is always a practice, not a final destination. In this case, knowledge about how your brain works gives you a foundation to awaken the energy of peace in you, to live a life with intention, and to give yourself permission to say "no" to anything currently present in your life that no longer serves you. This can include relationships, mindsets, projects, world-views, self-talk, or any other part of your life that makes you feel like less of yourself rather than more.

Throughout the rest of this book, we will look at many different tools and approaches that can be used to move from sympathetic dominance to parasympathetic dominance in our nervous systems. I take a holistic approach to this in order to help you understand yourself at the intersection between your thoughts, feelings, physical state, and connection to your divine nature.

Thoughts vs Feelings

The ability to embrace both peace and our humanity involves questioning thoughts that don't serve us while still allowing ourselves to feel every feeling. In order to do this, however, we must first make sure we understand the difference between a thought and a feeling. Sound simple? For most of us, it's usually not.

For example, if I were to ask you, *how do you feel about institutional racism?* You might respond, *It's wrong and we need to find solutions.* But this isn't really answering the question. The question is how you feel, which may be angry or sad or confused or helpless. We are trained by society and wired in our brains to find problems and their solutions, not to focus on how we're feeling about them. And yet, being able to be present with our feelings allows us to find clarity and wisdom (peace's close cousins) in any situation.

A thought is nothing more than words inside your head about what's going on in the world around you or inside yourself. A feeling, on the other hand, is an emotional state or reaction. For example, if you get in a fight with your best friend, you may experience being hurt, angry, upset, or confused. These are your feelings. You may also think things like, *she's way out of line* or *I can't believe she said that* or *she needs to understand I'm just trying to help.* These are your thoughts.

As we discussed earlier, our brains are designed to process information about the world around us, and our thoughts and feelings are both necessary to do that. Thoughts are harmless unless we get attached to them. When we believe our negative thoughts as truth, however, we can experience suffering because we are fighting against the reality of what is.[13] Feelings are also harmless— as long as we allow ourselves to feel them. However, when we do things to avoid feeling our feelings we experience suffering because we become disconnected from ourselves.

Thoughts often come with images, which are pictures in our heads about the thoughts. For example, if you think about giving a presentation at work, you may start to envision what that will look like. You can see yourself standing in front of a room full of people with sweaty palms and a pounding heart while you fumble over your words. You may also see painful images that go even further into the future such as yourself not getting the promotion you want-

---

[13] A great book with an elegant process for self-inquiry into any situation that is causing pain or suffering: Katie, B., S. Mitchell. 2002. *Loving What Is: Four Questions That Can Change Your Life.* New York: Three Rivers Press.

ed or defaulting on your student loans because you can no longer afford to pay them.

As these images materialize in your head, you will probably start to experience the symptoms of the anxiety you were imagining in real life. Your muscles tense and you suddenly feel an overwhelming sense of doom as the movie of your presentation blunder plays in your mind. This happens because your brain doesn't know the difference between imagining something terrible happening and it actually happening. The same neurochemicals get released and the same physical reactions take place.[14] So in this case, it wasn't the actual presentation that led to your anxiety about it—it was your thoughts about the presentation. And it wasn't a room full of people that caused your suffering—it was your own mind.

Most thoughts aren't objectively true or false. In other words, if you put your thought on trial, it would be hard for it to prove itself beyond a reasonable doubt in a court of law. Luckily, the most important aspect of a thought isn't whether it's true but whether it's helpful.

---

[14] This study describes the way our thoughts, emotions, and body feelings are linked through shared networks of neurons: Oosterwijk, S.,K. Lindquist, E. Anderson, R. Dautoff, Y. Moriguchi, L. Feldman Barrett. 2013. States of mind: Emotions, body feelings, and thoughts share distributed neural networks. Neuroimage. 2012 Sep; 62(3): 2110–2128. Published online 2012 Jun 5. doi: 10.1016/j.neuroimage.2012.05.079

How do you know if a thought is helpful? These questions might help:

- Does this thought support me to have more of what I want in my life (i.e. peace, meaning, purpose, love)?
- How do I feel when I have this thought?
- How do I act when I have this thought?
- Can the opposite of this thought be equally true or even truer? Can I find examples?
- What would my experience of the situation be like if I weren't having this negative thought about it?

It's a truth of the human experience that we're not supposed to feel good all the time. Yet although both positive and negative feelings are normal, we assume that the negative feelings are an indication that there's something wrong or something that needs to be fixed in our lives.

Sometimes this is the case. Sometimes, however, we're just feeling what we need to feel and in labeling it as "wrong" or "bad," we create bad feelings and suffering about it. You can see how this can lead to a downward spiral—we feel bad and then we feel bad about feeling bad and suddenly we're not experiencing our feelings, we're judging and resisting and getting stuck in our feelings.

Paradoxically, by giving ourselves permission to not have to be happy all the time and allowing ourselves to feel the full range of human emotions, we give ourselves incredible freedom. For most of us, it's a huge relief to be able to experience negative feelings without the belief that we have to fix ourselves or the world just because we're not feeling good. Having negative emotions doesn't mean there's something wrong with us or our lives. It just means we're human and normal.

Gratitude can be a great tool to help us think differently and focus on all the good in our lives, but it's unfair to expect ourselves to be deliberately all the time. Women in particular so often get caught up in how they think they should be feeling and beat themselves up when they believe their feelings are "wrong". They believe that if they're not in a state of perpetual joy and gratitude for all the blessings in their lives, it means they're unappreciative or they're doing life wrong.

The truth is that it's possible to feel both bad and grateful at the same. Moreover, by allowing ourselves to be present with whatever the present moment is bringing to us, we open ourselves up to appreciate all that's there without judgment that it should be different or we should be different.

Letting Go of Resistance

When we resist our negative feelings, we have a very different experience than when we accept them. Suffering comes when we believe an experience should be different than it is because resistance to reality is always painful. Instead, we can look at the places where we are experiencing suffering in our lives, and see them as opportunities for healing and growth.

Resistance can be about the big things: *I can't believe I'm getting a divorce* or about the small things: *Why is the service here so slow?!* The circumstances aren't as important as our reaction. When we're in resistance, we tend to stop listening to our own inner-wisdom. We do things that are not in alignment with the person we really are and naturally, our quality of life immediately goes down.

For example, it's a painful experience when I feel disconnected from any member of my family. And yet, when I decide that my daughters should move faster or listen to me the first time I ask them to do something, or that they should stop whining, I immediately start taking actions that do just that. I yell. I threaten to take away dessert or screen time. I tell them that they should be acting differently. And all of this has the unfortunate effect of creating separation and disconnection from them. I want them to feel bad for their behavior so they'll stop it, and whether or not I achieve my goal, I guarantee the result that I feel bad.

Maybe I shouldn't have yelled, I think. *I really need to be more patient.* And now the criticism has turned as inward to the exact degree it was once turned outward. It's not the way my daughters are acting causes my pain. It was my thoughts about how they're acting and the action I take as a result of those thoughts and then the negative thoughts I have on top of that lead to my pain.

In order to take actions that are in integrity, we have to be willing to feel all the feelings that come up in the course of living our lives. With my kids, that would look like not taking any action until I get clear on what I'm really thinking and why I'm thinking it. Sometimes that can be done during a quiet hour with my journal. More often, it has to happen in the moment as life continues to unfold around me.

For example, when I get exasperated with my daughters for not brushing their teeth the first time I ask them, I can take a moment to pause and get still. I can ask myself, *what's really the problem here*? Or, put another way, *where's the fear?* Maybe I'm afraid my daughter will miss the bus and I'll have to drop her off, making me late and looking unprofessional for my first client of the day. Or maybe I'm afraid the ignoring of my request is a sign of a bigger issue that I have no authority over my own kids or that there's something wrong with them. Or maybe I'm already worn out from worrying about other things that have nothing to do with my kids and so I react to their normal childhood behavior by taking it personally.

The moment I clear on what the situation is bringing up for me is the moment I become free. Creating space between my thoughts, my feelings, and my reactions allows me to pause and get in alignment with my intentions. That doesn't mean I'm not allowed to still be annoyed with my kids or to set boundaries and expectations with them about their behavior. It just means that when I do, I do it from a place of honesty to my true self. My highest self. My self that is connected to the divine within me and reacts to challenges in ways that are congruent with my dignity.

I can still expect my kids to follow my rules and still have consequences when they don't. After all, they need to learn how to take care of themselves and function in society. It's just that when I'm not taking my kids' behavior personally or getting wrapped up in my beliefs about what they should be doing, I can stay clear on my intention for the situation.

If the outcome I'm looking for is still not happening, I can have peace about *that* while parenting my kids in the best way I know how—I just don't have to lose myself in the process. By letting go of my attachment to a specific outcome happening when that outcome is beyond my control, I can focus my energy and my thoughts on what I really want for any situation with my daughters: connection. I don't need them to not whine about brushing their teeth to feel connected to them. Instead, I can choose to feel connected no matter what the external circumstances are.

Understanding this has been a huge relief.

Radical Self-Care

The universe is made of both light and dark, and so are we. Most of us embrace our light while having a contemptuous relationship with our dark sides because we believe that it represents all of our flaws. We equate our dark sides with pain, shame, and inadequacy. This view causes us to feel even more pain and shame and to unconsciously direct those feelings inward where they become a private source of daily suffering.

The truth is that it's impossible for dark to exist without light or for light to exist without dark. They define each other and although they are opposites, they're also allies. Without the negative, the positive would not exist. What makes a great day great is the fact that it is unique and special. Great days exist because we have the bad days and the so-so days to compare them to. Similarly, how would we know we're experiencing the feeling of joy if we don't have suffering and boredom and anger and sadness to compare it to and give it context?

Most of us realize this universal truth intellectually and yet we have trouble applying it to our daily experience. We believe that if we're not happy all the time, it means something has gone wrong in our lives. It's easy to forget that we're designed to have a full range of emotions, not just ones that feel good all the time. Yet the dark and the light together are what make us whole.

Radical self-care is about being willing to feel *all* our feelings and to make all our feelings welcome in our experience—even the negative ones. Especially the negative ones. This is because the more we are unwilling to experience a negative emotion such as anxiety, the more energy we give it and the stronger it gets.[15]

Being open to feeling all feelings and embracing all parts of ourselves is necessary to be able to live life fully and wholeheartedly. We can't have peace in our lives without also having deep compassion and gentle loving awareness for ourselves, for who we are, and what we're experiencing in the current moment.

Ironically, it's the labeling of parts of ourselves—including our emotions—as negative that ultimately keeps us stuck in them.[16]

---

[15] This is just one of many studies that show the more we try to suppress negative thoughts and emotions, the more intrusive they become: Marcks, B.A., and D.W. Woods. 2005. A comparison of thought suppression to an acceptance-based technique in the management of personal intrusive thoughts: A controlled evaluation. *Behavior Research and Therapy* 43:433-445.

[16] A great article that explains precisely how this ironic effect works in our brains in a variety of situations such as being unable to fall asleep when trying to fall asleep or feeling more of a negative mood when trying to feel less of it. Wegner, D. M. 1994. Ironic processes of mental control. *Psychological Review*. 101:34-52.

When we let go of the judgment, we let go of the suffering that is attached to them.

Doing this can be difficult, not in the sense that it requires a lot of energy, but in the sense that it can be tricky. This is because our negative feelings like to convince us of their truth. Our belief in their truth allows them to continue to exist, and as we discussed earlier, our fight-or-flight sympathetic nervous systems want the fearful thoughts to exist in order to protect us and keep us safe from potential threats.

This is why while part of radical self-care is allowing ourselves to feel every feeling, another crucial part is questioning every thought that doesn't serve us. We know if a thought is no longer serving us because it feels incongruent with our authentic selves. In other words, it feels like it's holding us back or no longer protecting us. It's not helping us to process an experience or make sense of something. It just feels bad and keeps us stuck. If this is the case, we can exercise our power of free will to make changes that do feel more in alignment.

What are negative thoughts that *do* feel congruent with our authentic selves? Sometimes something bad happens and we don't want to think ourselves out of feeling bad about it. When a loved one dies, we feel bad, and we don't want to not feel bad or to be indifferent about it.

Those reactions would feel incongruent. Sometimes we feel hurt by someone and we don't want to "just get over it." So we take care of ourselves by feeling all the feelings that go along with our experience including pain, grief, sadness, confusion, or anger.

We do this until we come to a place where we want to start thinking about the situation differently. Then we do.

Self-care of any kind is never earned or given. It always has to be claimed. Radical self-care requires that you answer the question *am I worth doing this for*. Am I worth feeling temporarily uncomfortable? Am I worth doing things I don't necessarily feel like doing at the moment because they're an indispensable part of being a person who lives my values?

Radical self-care is about loving yourself enough to live on purpose and with purpose. It's about saying "no" to the discomfort that comes when we tell ourselves we're not good enough and "yes" to the discomfort that comes when we become intentional with our thoughts and actions.

Our Two Emotions

Just as we're made of both light and dark as well as infinite shades of gray, we also have the two foundational emotions of love and fear, as well as many other emotions that are simply variations of those two. When we find ourselves in a negative thought process, stressing about something or someone beyond our control, making self-defeating choices, staying in toxic situations or relationships, or engaging in behaviors that have a net-negative effect (such as overeating, over-drinking, over screen-ing), it usually means we're acting from fear.

Some of the most common fears women experience are:

- Being unsafe (physically, psychologically, financially, even existentially)
- Being unloved
- Not having enough
- Not doing or being enough
- Being trapped or stuck in a painful situation
- Being out of control

- Losing oneself

- Being alone or abandoned

- Losing the people or things one loves the most

- Being inherently flawed

These fears can lead women to engage in negative cycles where they find themselves repeating patterns that keep them stuck in the very things they most want to avoid in life. Unfortunately, it's human nature that most of the time, we engage in these negative cycles with a complete lack of awareness for our own role in it. After all, the brain does not like to spontaneously change its entire worldview. Instead, it likes to establish a way of perceiving reality and stick with it—even if that perception is painful. It will then selectively interpret information to reinforce that worldview and prove itself right.[17] Our brains have evolved to keep us as safe as possible while exerting the least amount of energy (in itself important for survival).

Our negative cycles are in general born of our past hurts and traumas (in addition to our personalities and genes). When the sympathetic nervous system is activated, our brains do their best to

---

[17] This is called confirmation bias. An interesting collection of studies on how confirmation bias works: Nickerson, R. 1998. Confirmation bias: A Ubiquitous phenomenon in many guises. *Review of General Psychology.* Vol. 2 No. 2. 175-220.

protect us by making sure we're vigilant about avoiding that source of pain in the future.

In the primitive logic of our brains, living in the hurts of our past and worrying about being hurt the future allow us to survive the present. When we look at fear in this way, we can see it not as something to avoid or to "get over." After all, experiencing fear is just one of the things that makes us human. We don't need to escape our humanness. Rather, we can see fear as a messenger, a guide, a partner, and a completely normal experience.

Much in the same way the lungs are an organ designed to draw in oxygen and expel carbon dioxide in order to keep us alive, our brains are an organ designed to find problems and to solve those problems in order to keep us alive. Registering something as a problem usually involves feeling fear about it. This is the brain's way of motivating us to protect ourselves from the problem and ensure safety.

It's natural to label as a problem anything that causes a negative emotion for us. This can include mundane things —like your neighbor parking in your spot, as well as significant things—like the death of a loved one. We think that if people or situations are causing our negative feelings and are therefore a problem, we need to fix the people and the situations. And if bad things are happening in the world, that's a problem we take on as needing to change too.

In the world we live in, it's easy to get into this frame of mind, and easy to find problems wherever we look. We see something that we define as unjust or unfair and we try to change it. We argue with people, with situations, with reality, and when that fails, we feel defeated and believe we now have justification to feel bad.

The way to override the snowball of pain our fearful thoughts cause is to step into the present moment and sit with openness and curiosity about what we uncover there. Only then do we become able to see our thoughts with clarity. Seeing with clarity gives us the gift of knowledge and understanding—of ourselves and of the deeper world around us, and in this, we find freedom and we find peace.

I'm writing this at 2:30 in the afternoon and I can't even count the number of times I've already argued with reality today, but here are a few examples:

- Someone I care about died last week and I can't stop thinking about it. *It shouldn't have happened. She should still be here. What if? What if? What if?* I feel fear: fear about the fact that death can happen to anyone, at any time, and fear about how her family is coping.

These thoughts have been consuming me. I know it's my brain's way of trying to solve the problem of missing her, and that missing her is a problem with no solution. I know grief has a purpose and it isn't supposed to feel good, but that doesn't make it feel any less painful.

- I pulled my neck at the gym and it hurts every time I move it in a certain direction.[18] I keep thinking about ways to fix it—heating pads, essential oils, hot baths, magnesium spray, massages. My brain doesn't like pain and it wants it stopped immediately. I'm afraid I really screwed up my back and it will require extensive medical intervention to get better.

- I opened a cabinet this morning and saw that I forgot to add an ingredient to the soup I made and served to my friends last night. I felt compelled to text them and apologize for my error so they would know I'm normally a better soup maker than

---

[18] In retrospect, it's probably not a coincidence that I learned of the loss of someone I cared about and then a few days later hurt my neck at the gym. As mentioned in an earlier footnote, the brain shares common circuitry for physical pain and emotional pain.

our meal last night would suggest. Fear drove me to do it—the fear that someone would think less of me because of a subpar soup and the fear that the evening was somehow diminished because of it.

- My four-year-old daughter fell on the driveway and scraped her hands and knees. She was screaming bloody murder and I was trying to comfort her. I wanted her to feel better, but I also really wanted the screaming to stop as quickly as possible because the sound of screaming children is overwhelming and anxiety-producing for me. Perhaps this is a more primal fear—the fear every parent automatically feels when they have a screaming child on their hands.

So what's the answer? Do we give up and resign ourselves to the fact that our lives are full of problems that cause us to feel fear and there's nothing we can do to stop it? Do we just stop caring and allow ourselves to become indifferent?

I believe there is another path—one that doesn't require we bury our heads in the sand or become a punching bag, but also doesn't require that we feel bad in order to make things better. It just requires that we change the goal from ridding ourselves of problems and the feelings of fear they cause to being curious and open to about how we can befriend them. When this happens, we begin to see our fear not as an adversary but as our teacher and healer.

I've been actively on a journey to allow more peace into my life since college, and I can say that a lot of the time, my brain is still in problem-solving/fear mode. But I can also say that it is much better than it was ten years ago, five years ago, even last week. The more I see my feelings of fear as fellow travelers on my human journey, the more I can practice openness and curiosity with them.

Little by little, the less I see my problems as sources of suffering to be fixed or eliminated from my life and the more I see them as there to serve my growth and evolution, the more I can connect to peace. And so even though much of the time I still find a way to deny peace to myself, through acceptance I've luckily found peace about *that*.

Finding Authenticity

As a child, my client Danielle had always been called "shy." She did not actually feel shy but rather felt overwhelmed by over-eager strangers who came on too strongly. However, since it was adults that were telling her she was shy, she took their labels at face value and began to internalize the belief that she was in fact shy.

As she grew older, Danielle started to recognize that in society, shyness is generally viewed as a negative trait. She would hear "don't be shy" or "oh she's shy!" from adults (who were probably just projecting their own social discomforts onto her) and she would understand that "shy" was not only something that defined her, it was also a problem that needed fixing.

By her teenage years, this label started to cause Danielle anxiety. In high school, she felt increasingly awkward and uncomfortable in any situation where she might be around people she didn't know. She worried about what to say and how to say it. She felt like she never said the right things and believed people were judging her as "awkward" or "weird." Around people she knew, she was able to be herself—a self that was actually quite comfortable engaging with others, but outside a small group of close friends, she felt deeply flawed and embarrassed.

By the time she was an adult, Danielle had developed full-blown Social Anxiety Disorder, a diagnosable mental health condition in which a person experiences significant anxiety and distress in social settings where they feel observed, noticed, or scrutinized.[19]

Danielle's quality of life was now significantly impacted. She couldn't go to a business meeting without feeling a pit in her stomach, sweaty palms, and an overall feeling of dread. She obsessively worried about what her colleagues would think of her if she didn't know what to say or said the wrong thing. Not surprisingly, the experience of social anxiety severely affected her self-esteem, which only served to deepen the anxiety itself. The entire thing became a self-perpetuating cycle that Danielle saw no way out of.

---

[19] How shame and Social Anxiety Disorder are connected and how cognitive behavioral therapy, the type of therapy I use in this example, is shown to be an effective treatment: Hedman, E., P. Ström, A. Stünkel, E. Mörtberg. 2013. Shame and guilt in social anxiety disorder: Effects of cognitive behavior therapy and association with social anxiety and depressive symptoms. *Plos One* https://doi.org/10.1371/journal.pone.0061713

My work with Danielle took three paths that regularly intertwined. The first was helping her to stop judging herself and to stop wishing she was someone different. This was tricky because she had long assumed there was something deeply flawed about her—something that needed fixing but that might ultimately be unfixable.[20] She was terrified that her flaws kept her from the deep connection she craved with others and ultimately doomed her to a life of loneliness and inadequacy.

Danielle hated the part of herself that felt awkward around people she didn't know. She also hated the anxiety that caused the feeling of awkwardness. She was embarrassed by the anxiety and truly believed she was the only one at her company who struggled the way she did. Everyone else seemed to enjoy themselves at events. Everyone else seemed cool, calm and collected during meetings. Why couldn't she?

I pointed out to Danielle that while she constantly feared being rejected by others, the one who was by far rejecting her the most was herself. If she wanted the feeling of being accepted, the easiest place to start would be to give acceptance to herself instead of waiting for someone else to give it to her. This was a new way of thinking for Danielle who

---

[20] These feelings reflect shame researcher Brené Brown's definition of shame: "An intensely painful feeling or experience of believing we are flawed and therefore unworthy of acceptance of belonging." Brown, B. 2006. Shame resilience theory: A grounded theory study on women and shame. *Families in Society: The Journal of Contemporary Social Services.* 87: 43-52.

had long believed that if she accepted the parts of herself that caused her pain, it would she was giving up on any chance of changing them.

I helped Danielle to really question the notion that there was anything wrong with her at all. A state of self-acceptance would in fact be a much stronger foundation for showing up in the world in ways that felt authentic than a state of shame. There could still always be areas where she could choose to learn and grow—such as enhancing her social and conversational skills or learning tools to better manage her anxiety, but none of those things was a requirement for being "worthy" or for "fixing" herself.

As Danielle began to change her mindset and let go of her long-held belief that she was a flawed person, she began to recognize that she was exactly who she was supposed to be. She was able to embrace that she was naturally an introvert and would always get her energy from deeper, more meaningful connections with others. In this, she gave herself permission to stop comparing herself to extroverts and began to let go of the self-hatred she had carried with her for so many years.

It was a relief to realize that not being comfortable in social situations was a problem for Danielle only because she believed it to be—not because of some incontrovertible truth. Therefore, she didn't need to change herself, she only needed to change her beliefs about herself. Paradoxically, this shift in her thinking helped Danielle to feel more comfortable in her own skin, which naturally had the effect of putting her more at ease around others.

Instead of trying to escape her flaws to avoid the suffering she believed they were causing, Danielle moved more into alignment with her authentic self—a self that preferred intimate connection but was also able to engage in social situations with people she didn't know with a greater sense of peace and autonomy. As she embraced who she was and how she most enjoyed showing up in the world and with others, she was able to stop pressuring herself to be someone she wasn't while at the same time, developing an honest and compassionate relationship with the woman she was.

The second step for Danielle was realizing that her anxiety had, as most of our emotions do, become self-perpetuating.[21] The more she worried about having it, the more it seemed to be there. The fear of the anxiety was rooted in a belief that it would rob her of the things she wanted most in life, that it would cause her embarrassment, and that it would only continue to get worse and more difficult to handle as time went on. Ironically, it wasn't the anxiety that

---

[21] When it comes to emotions, what we resist persists.

was hanging these threats over her head. It was the fearful thinking about the anxiety that was.

Danielle began to shift her mindset and to trust that there was no emotion she couldn't survive— even panic. She was able to recognize that she wasn't her anxiety. Anxiety was just a label she was giving to a series of feelings she was having in her body and thoughts she was having in her mind. Her mindset shifted more and more as she started to look at the anxiety without judgment or resistance. This allowed her to connect more with the part of herself that was observing the anxiety and less with the part that was experiencing it. It also allowed Danielle to give herself permission to feel other "negative" feelings she had been avoiding out of fear that they were wrong or that they would overwhelm her like anger, sadness, and even boredom.

The third step for Danielle was to learn tools to be able to challenge the negative thoughts she had about herself and about the anxiety she experienced, to de-activate her sympathetic nervous system whenever she needed to with mindfulness and meditation, and to restructure her life so that there was plenty of margin to decompress, especially during periods of high stress. All these tools were ways of making peace with anxiety and developing a practice of self-love and self-compassion.

Danielle now understood that the greatest block to her peace wasn't some unfixable character flaw. It wasn't even the anxiety. It was her unwillingness to allow what she was experiencing to be there without judgment or struggle.[22] The goal was no longer to get rid of anxiety or to become immune to it. The goal was to realize that peace was an option no matter what external or internal experience she was having.

Not only that, Danielle also discovered that the peace she had so desperately been seeking was inside her the whole time. It was the divine in her—a treasure that was always present, and once found can never be lost. Now the dark was no longer an obstacle to the light. It was a catalyst to remember the light in her and to help her experience the light (her essential nature) in new ways.

---

[22] This study involved giving high anxiety females two 10-minute periods of 10% carbon dioxide enriched air, before which they received training to either try to mindfully observe or try to control symptoms via diaphragmatic breathing. A third group received no instruction. The ones who were trained in mindful observation had less panic-related symptoms than the ones who tried to control their symptoms or the ones who were left to their own devices. This study certainly speaks to the effectiveness of mindful observation in reducing symptoms of anxiety, though I must say, I had a bit of anxiety in just reading what the study participants had to go through! Eifert, G. H. and M. Heffner. 2003. The effects of acceptance versus control contexts on avoidance of panic-related symptoms. *Journal of Experimental Analysis of Behavior*. 73:5-22.

Our Brains Work Like This

This how our brains work:

1. We have an experience (something outside or inside us happens).

2. We have thoughts about the experience.

   This is where our brain does its job of keeping us safe by explaining, evaluating, comparing, categorizing, fixing, and/or judging the experience. It does this based on every other event we have consciously or subconsciously experienced in our lives. In other words, our thoughts are really just a collection of words and symbols to help us process information that happens almost all the time and automatically.

3. We have feelings about the thoughts.

   If we believe a negative thought to be true, we feel bad. If we believe a positive thought to be true, we feel good, and vice versa. There are three problems with this:

- We are terrible judges of whether our thoughts reflect reality—they seem true to us, but that's only because we're the ones thinking them.

- Having and believing a negative thought about a current experience influences our future experience, which only reinforces our biased beliefs.

- Brain cells that fire together wire together:[23] the wiring in the brain can easily make negative connections that may or may not be objectively true. The brain is also very good at putting a lot of intensity and energy into convincing us that it's right.

4. We take action based on our thoughts and our feelings.

If we are thinking fearful thoughts and feeling fearful feelings, it becomes very difficult to take actions that are congruent with our highest, most authentic selves. Instead, we take actions that create results that reinforce our negative bias.

---

[23] This principle is called Hebbian Theory. Here's more on how it works: Keysers, C., and V. Gazzola. 2014. Hebbian learning and predictive mirror neurons for actions, sensations, and emotions. Philosophical Transactions of the Royal Society Publishing. 2014 June 5; 369(1644): 20130175. doi: 10.1098/rstb.2013.0175

Thinking about our brains in this way, it becomes clear that if we don't create some distance between ourselves and our thoughts, we are doomed to get stuck in negative patterns we can't see.

One way to begin to create space between our thoughts and our emotions is to consciously change the language we use in our thinking. Doing this allows us to introduce awareness and intention into beliefs and behaviors that were previously automatic and unconscious. The net result is that we give ourselves margin to turn off the sympathetic nervous system, get clear on our intentions for the situation, and get in integrity with ourselves before we react.

For example, the thought, "I'm so anxious" is one that for most of us, creates more feelings of anxiety in the thinking of it. This is because in this thought, there is no separation between our experience of the anxiety and ourselves.[24] When we have the thought, "I'm so anxious," and we believe it, the anxiety becomes a very unwelcome and feared part of us.

The idea that anxiety is something we can't escape because it's literally a part of who we are is a terrifying one for sure. It brings with it

---

[24] The book, *The Untethered Soul* does a wonderful job of describing how to separate your identity from your thoughts. I highly recommend it. Singer, M. A. (2007). *The untethered soul: The journey beyond yourself.* Oakland, CA: New Harbinger Publications.

images of being stuck, helpless, powerless, and victimized by something we have no control over. The feeling of anxiety can certainly be a painful and unpleasant one, but it's our thoughts about the feeling that creates a self-fulfilling and self-reinforcing prophecy. All of this is, of course, incompatible with the feeling of peace we all desire.

On the other hand, the thought, "I'm having a feeling and I'm labeling that feeling as anxiety," is different. In this case, the thinker is acknowledging the feeling and allowing herself to feel it, but she isn't attaching her identity to it. She is allowing it to exist and allowing herself to note and feel its existence, but she is not mistaking herself for the feeling.

When it comes to our emotional and thought cycles, peace becomes both an action and a state of mind. We let go of our judgments and allow each feeling, each experience, to just be what it is. We do this knowing that everything in life is temporary. Painful feelings and experiences are a part of life, but they are never the full story. No matter what our external circumstances are, there is always free will in our minds and there is always the opportunity to shift our perception of a situation that is causing us suffering. The space between our thinking and our thoughts is where peace can be found for all of us.

I was at my local mall a few days ago buying a new knife at Williams Sonoma. It was the start of the holiday season, and the stores were mobbed with people. I got on what appeared to be the checkout line and asked the woman in front of me if it was, in fact, the checkout line. She told me that it was. I then proceeded to wait a full ten minutes while the people in front of me were very slowly checked out. When the next register opened I started to walk toward it, but someone went in front of me.

"Excuse me, I was next," I said.

"No, you weren't. The line starts here." I turned to see a long line of people waiting several feet away. The person who had spoken was a man in his early 20's. "That's not the line there," he added rather loudly.

"I was told the line was here and I've been waiting ten minutes," I replied.

"Well, that's too bad. That's not the line so you're going to have to go to the back! You're not cutting in front of all of us." he said nastily. I was completely taken off guard that someone would speak to a stranger that way. I looked him in the eye for a moment while I weighed my options on what to do next.

Finally, I said, "I'm not going to do that."

He condescendingly shrugged his shoulders at me and said, "well, I guess you're not shopping here today," then turned away to talk to the man he was standing with.

My heart pounded in my chest and my cheeks flushed as I stood frozen in place for a second trying to decide what to do. There was no way I was going to the back of the line, but I certainly didn't want to escalate this humiliating interaction about it either. I felt shamed standing there having been loudly yelled at for my mistake, and angry at this guy for designating himself the checkout line authority and then feeling the need to publicly embarrass me. I was also bewildered as to how a seemingly innocuous interaction with a stranger had escalated to this point so quickly.

Luckily, before the awkward situation went any further, the woman at the front of the line offered to let me go ahead of her. "This line is so confusing," she said kindly.

After I left the mall, I couldn't stop thinking about what had happened. I kept replaying it in my mind and every time I did, I would feel a pit in my stomach, my heart would start to pound, and I would literally be on the verge of tears. Admittedly, I may have been feeling things a bit more intensely because I was stressed out and hormonal, but I'm also just a sensitive person and being yelled at by a stranger in a public place is never going to be a pleasant experience for me.

That evening, I told my husband about the situation and he reminded me that the one who should have been embarrassed was the guy making a scene in Williams Sonoma, not me. But still, I felt awful every time I thought about it and wondered if I should have reacted differently.

Should I have said something like, "That was really uncalled for," to the guy? Should I have asked him why he was yelling at me? In reality, I knew it made no sense to continue reliving what amounted to two minutes of discomfort, but that didn't stop me from thinking about it over and over again. My brain didn't care if it made sense or if it was over and done with. My brain wanted to keep reliving it and it wanted to get upset every time it did.

Eventually, I decided that if my brain wanted to make peace with this situation, I needed to allow myself to feel whatever I needed to feel about it but still do some inquiry into my thoughts about it. Compassion is a necessary component of peace[25] and so I started by challenging myself to think about the guy who had been nasty to me with as much compassion as I wished he had given me in the line.

If he was speaking to a random stranger like that in front of a bunch of random strangers, it probably meant he had been spoken to like that himself at some point in his life. Maybe for him, it wasn't a random stranger, it was someone he loved. Or many someones he loved. Or both someone he loved and also random strangers multiple times in different ways.

Maybe he was feeling out of control in a significant area in his life or was having anxiety about waiting on a long line in a crowded store, and micromanaging it was his way of desperately grasping at peace in his chaotic world. Maybe he really thought I was someone who was trying to cheat the system by jumping ahead in line and he thought he was helping everyone else in line out by putting me in my place.

---

[25] It's a necessary component of peace in our own minds and also in the world. This article argues that if issues of social justice and decrease the prevalence of suffering and injustice in Western society, we must create a collective value framework based on compassion. The article also describes how perceptions of likeness and difference as well as desert and responsibility can be impediments to compassion. I believe this model can be applied to our daily interactions with others like with mine and the guy at Williams Sonoma, on a societal level in our policies and social constructs, and on a personal level with ourselves. Williams, C. 2008. Compassion, suffering and the self: A moral psychology of social justice. *Current Sociology.* 56(1): 5-24. https://doi.org/10.1177%2F0011392107084376

No matter what his motivation, he was clearly a man who was living in a world where yelling at a stranger on a checkout line at the mall was a legitimate response to a situation. And for that, I could have compassion. I could also develop compassion by remembering all the times I had wrongly accused someone of something—either in my mind or out loud, and hurt them in the process.

In thinking about it, I couldn't name one relationship where I hadn't at one point or another reacted with anger only to later deeply regret my behavior and come to the conclusion that it was completely uncalled for. I had assumed the worst about both loved ones and strangers more times than I could count. Many of those times I had also called them out for it in a way I later felt terrible for.

I remember a time many years ago when I was living in New York City and my boyfriend, Chris, who later became my husband, and I had been dating for about a year. We were out with friends from grad school and I misread a situation and accused him of something that he immediately denied. This led to a fight on the subway that lasted all the way from lower Manhattan to Queens.

The fight was finally resolved when I came to the painful and embarrassing conclusion that it was literally impossible for him to have done the thing I was accusing him of. In retrospect, I realized that I had created a story in my head that he was untrustworthy, then jumped on what I thought was an example of it because I was afraid that if I got too close I would be hurt. Luckily, Chris forgave me quickly. It took much longer for me to forgive myself.

When I think about it with open-mindedness and compassion, I can see that what led me to yell at the guy I loved was the same thing that led the guy on the Williams Sonoma line to yell at me: fear. This makes his reaction human, and it makes mine human too. In that way, he and I are very much the same. We're not bad people. We're just people whose nervous systems get overwhelmed sometimes and this causes us to act in ways that come at the expense of our own peace.

Accepting Acceptance

I read a story a while back, though I don't recall where, about two families who both lost their homes in a hurricane. When a TV news crew came to the street where the neighborhood was assessing the damage, they interviewed the first family who said, "We lost everything—our house and everything in it is gone." The family was understandably overwhelmed by the loss of their home and all of their worldly possessions.

Moving further down the street, the news crew interviewed a second family who said, "We lost our house and our stuff but we have everything—we are all safe and okay and everything that's irreplaceable in our lives is still right here. The rest we can figure out."

The thing about the story that struck me was that two families could go through the exact same devastating, traumatic experience on the same day and yet have two very different reactions. That doesn't mean the second family didn't feel anxiety, sadness, anger, or trauma. I'm sure they did. These are human reactions to losing your home and your belongings, and it would make sense for the family to allow themselves to feel these feelings fully. It just means they were also able to shift their focus and consider all the aspects of the experience they found themselves in—the painful and the peaceful.

We can decide that we'll have peace when things go the way we think they should, or we can decide that we want our peace to be our own and nothing outside ourselves can keep us from it. Things happen in life but having free will means we get to decide what they mean.[26] The worst thing that can happen to us is never the thing itself—it's what we think and feel about it.

Courtney had a long-standing issue with her mother-in-law, Joanne who lived in the same town as Courtney and her family and so would often stop by unannounced to visit with the grandkids. Courtney found Joanne to be snarky and disrespectful of her parenting. She would communicate to Joanne that she didn't want her children to be given unhealthy, processed foods or watch more than an hour of TV when they visited their grandmother, and would later find out those wishes were completely ignored.

---

[26] A remarkable book by Viktor Frankl, a psychiatrist who survived Nazi concentration camps while his entire family was killed and his life's work lost. A phenomenal work on the ways we find can find meaning in life and how your freedom to choose how you respond to a situation is the one thing that can never be taken away from you: Frankl, V. 1962. *Man's Search for Meaning*. Boston: Beacon Press.

Joanne made backhanded comments about Courtney's desire to work instead of stay home with the kids, was constantly complaining about her own life, and always seemed to play the part of the victim in every story she told. Joanne was divorced and retired and did not have many friends, and so she had a habit of inviting herself along to family outings where she would complain about the service in restaurants and stores and talk down to waiters and salespeople while Courtney cringed. Courtney's husband Dave felt uncomfortable saying "no" to his mother, and the times he did, Joanne made it clear it made her feel disrespected by giving him the silent treatment for several weeks.

Although Courtney had no problem not speaking to Joanne for several weeks, it made her angry that her husband was being treated that way by his mother. At the same time, Courtney was also starting to resent her husband for not standing up to his mother more and not creating better boundaries between her and their family.

One day Courtney decided to host a party at her home and invite all her closest friends and coworkers plus her sisters and some cousins. Wanting to enjoy the party—a rare time where all her favorite people would be under the same roof having fun, Courtney, of course, did not mention the party to Joanne and specifically planned the party for a weekend when Joanne was supposed to be away visiting her other son and his husband.

However, an hour into the party, Joanne showed up at Courtney's house and explained that she cut the visit with her son short because his husband had said something to offend her. Seeing the crowd of people and the food over Courtney's shoulder, she asked Courtney if she could come in. Courtney felt stuck. The last person she wanted at a party for all her favorite people was her mother-in-law, but Courtney knew if she didn't allow Joanne to come in, there would surely be drama about it later. Still, work on boundaries had given Courtney the strength to say "no" to things that didn't feel right for her regardless of how the other person felt about it.

I had been encouraging Courtney to experiment with challenging her thinking about situations that were causing her distress—not to change her mind, but to see if more peace was possible for her no matter what the external circumstances were. Courtney decided to see this particular conundrum as an opportunity to try the experiment: she would see if she could let Joanne into her home but not into her mind.

Courtney knew she had the option to say "no" to Joanne, but that doing so would not prevent Joanne from taking up valuable space in her mind during the party. In fact, it would do the opposite. She knew she would obsess about whether she had made the right decision and rage about Joanne's overbearing personality. She would spend the party perseverating about her relationship with her mother-in-law instead of enjoying her relationships with the people she loved to be with and who were all in her house at that very moment.

Courtney decided that she was willing to say "yes" to Joanne coming into her home during her party not because she wasn't honoring her own boundaries, but because she was. Courtney was tired of living in a world where one person had the power to ruin the best parts of her life.

In our work together, Courtney had recently come to the realization that she wanted to control her mother-in-law as much as her mother-in-law wanted to control her. Courtney wanted Joanne to be different than she was. She wanted Joanne to have an entirely different personality and she had convinced herself that she couldn't be happy unless this happened. Courtney realized that she was doing as much judging and complaining as her mother-in-law; the only difference was Courtney was doing it in her mind and behind Joanne's back to anyone who would listen, and Joanne did it directly to the person's face.

Courtney understood that she had become a catalyst of her own suffering. And Courtney didn't want to suffer any more about this. She came to the conclusion that if she only allowed herself to feel peace when Joanne was behaving the way she wanted her to, then Courtney would be the one depriving herself of peace—not Joanne. Joanne, Courtney realized, was just being Joanne. She wasn't trying to be obnoxious or difficult to be around. In fact, in Joanne's mind, acting the way she did was probably completely logical and justified.

At the same time, Courtney also had to let go of the fear that allowing Joanne to join the party would mean she couldn't continue to exercise whatever boundaries felt right for her in the future. She decided her boundaries could evolve as she did, and allowing something to happen once didn't have to mean she was now committed to allowing it to it happening forever. Since Courtney had told herself that this was just an experiment, she was willing to temporarily let go of the notion that Joanne would mistakenly get the message her behavior was okay or that she was being forgiven for every hurt she ever caused Courtney and her husband in the past.

Courtney found that it was a major relief to temporarily let go of the anger and resentment she had previously believed to not be optional. It felt good to know that she wasn't stuck in thoughts that caused suffering—that those thoughts were a choice and she could always choose to think differently if it felt right to do so. This gave her permission to have peace in the moment and not be overtaken by grudges about Joanne's behavior in the past or fears about reinforcing her behavior in the future.

To Courtney's surprise, when she gave herself the mental space to have the experience that was already unfolding instead of resenting that she wasn't having a different, better one, she was able to more fully enjoy herself. There were still moments at the party where she felt the need to roll her eyes at Joanne, but for the most part, she was able to be present with her friends and family and to deeply enjoy the moment with them instead of being off in her own world, silently fuming. It was much more peaceful for her to focus on the many guests she was thrilled to be there instead of the one guest she didn't want.

Through this experience, Courtney learned a lesson about the space between resistance and peace. If she tried to deny Joanne the experience of the party, Courtney would have automatically denied herself the experience as well. As soon as she confronted Joanne, she would be doing something that was no longer fun, and for Courtney at least, the party would be over. The energy of the party would likely also shift, and so for the guests, the party might go from enjoyable to awkward. Whether Courtney was "right" in this situation or not was irrelevant to her having peace in it. The bottom line was that she couldn't have both resentment and peace at the same time. She made a choice in this situation, and she chose herself.

This is how all of us are: when we attempt to resist, ignore, or buffer our feelings, they seem to get bigger and more powerful because we're giving them more of our energy. Instead, we can allow ourselves to be human and to feel all feelings whether positive or negative and yet still maintain sovereignty over how we react to those feelings.

Most of us believe that pain and peace are incongruent—if we're in physical or emotional pain, we cannot have peace at the same time. I want to offer that pain and peace can coexist. It's suffering and peace that are incongruent. So much of our suffering is the result of buying into thoughts about how things should be different and deciding that we can't find peace until they are. Luckily, we do have at least some control over our suffering. While pain is a feeling—a physical or emotional response—suffering comes from our thoughts about what we feel. We might not be able to feel differently (nor would we always want to), but we can always choose to think differently.

Being connected to peace means we are willing to feel hopelessness, panic, rage, and all other feelings that we would normally not want to allow ourselves to feel.[27] We do this knowing that there's no emotion

---

[27] Much more about willingness to feel negative feelings can be found in this book: KabatZinn, J. 2013. *Full Catastrophe Living: Using the Wisdom of Your Body and Mind to Face Stress, Pain, and Illness.* New York: Bantam Books.

we can't survive and that all emotions are temporary. Being connected to peace also means we do not label ourselves as "weak" for not feeling the way we believe we're supposed to in a given situation. To allow peace in the present moment, no matter what that present moment brings to us—this is where we find wholeheartedness, consciousness, confidence, and connection to our inner-wisdom.

In other words, this is where we find ourselves.

A Note on Accepting and Indifference,

Pain and Suffering

Many of my clients believe that if they accept something, it will mean they've given up or no longer care about it. But there is a difference between accepting something and being indifferent to it. Indifference is about denial while accepting is about transcendence. Acceptance is about seeing things as they actually are, not getting stuck in how we believe they "should" be.[28] This doesn't mean letting go of caring about the things that are important to us. It simply means being with what is and letting go of the suffering that comes when we deny, struggle against, or resist reality.

I find that this is an area where my clients struggle a lot. And I get it. For much of my life, I just assumed that if I didn't want something to be the way it was, I needed to be upset about it in order to change it. Not being upset felt like the equivalent of condoning it. For example,

---

[28] More about this in: Kabat-Zinn, J. 2005. *Wherever You Go, There You Are.* New York: Hachette Books.

if I didn't get angry when someone cuts me off on the highway, it meant I was indifferent to bad drivers on the road. How could I accept people doing dangerous things that could affect innocent lives? Anger felt both justified and right—even if I knew logically that my anger had zero impact on the driving habits of strangers.

I can now see, however, that accepting bad drivers doesn't mean I condone them or don't think it would be a good thing if they changed the way they drive. It just means I don't see value in getting enraged when I see one. I can still take effective action (like report the license plate) if I see someone is truly doing something unsafe and I feel the need to do something about it. It's not that I'm indifferent to bad drivers. It's just that I'm willing to accept that I live in a world where bad drivers do exist and no amount of anger on my part will change that fact.

Acceptance doesn't mean abandoning what I think is right or that I somehow trick myself into feeling good about things my value system disagrees with. I'll never feel good about murder or sexual assault or child hunger or animal abuse or environmental devastation. But not allowing my emotional state to be completely disturbed by these things allows me to live with more peace and also enables me to take action with greater clarity and understanding of what reality is.

If I want more peace in myself and in the world, it is crazy for me to think that uncontrolled anger and outrage will ever be the way to get there. Peace is something you either have in the present moment—no matter what the present moment holds—or you don't. Peace is never something you get to by mentally fighting with the things you believe are blocking it from you. It is possible to allow ourselves to have peace and still take intelligent, thoughtful action toward positive change in our lives and in the world.

Another example where we can see and understand the distinction between acceptance and indifference is in getting older and dying. We are all aware that as time passes, we get older. This is true for every living being on the planet. The minute we're born, we start to age, and for all of us, life will ultimately end with death. Fearing death doesn't change the fact that with 100% certainty, it will definitely happen to us and to everyone we know.

Accepting that we will all get old and die eventually (or possibly die before we're old) doesn't mean we are indifferent to this fact. Most of us accept death as an inevitably and yet still take some steps to live a full, healthy life like eating healthy foods and seeking medical treatment when we're sick. Just because taking care of ourselves isn't a permanent solution to prevent death or aging, it doesn't mean that it's not something that's worthwhile to do for a variety of reasons.

At the same time, being terrified or panicked by the thought of death does nothing to stop it from happening either. We can mentally resist it all we want, but mental resistance to something we don't want is useless in stopping it from happening. Instead, we can see death for what it is and yet still take action that is aligned with our values to have a positive impact—not necessarily on how or when we ultimately experience death, but on how we experience life in the present moment.

The same applies to all areas of our lives where we experience resistance to reality. Even politics. Even difficult people. Accepting these things doesn't mean we don't try to mitigate their impact on our lives and the lives of others. I can accept that there will be many political issues I believe in that will not go the way I want them to, but at no point does that also have to mean I'm satisfied with the way things are or that I tolerate injustice.

Similarly, I can accept that a family member or colleague is who they are and I can decide not to base my happiness on my belief that they should change, and still, I can consistently set boundaries with them. This principle is also true on a larger scale with the greatest sources of suffering in the human experience—war, trauma, hunger, hatred, violence. We can accept them as a part of the collective human experience and let go of our internal anger about the fact that they exist in the world, yet still actively try to stop ourselves and others from experiencing them and stop those who are perpetrators.

While this concept is easy to understand in theory, it can be much more tricky to put into practice. It's natural to feel like accepting something is equivalent to condoning or even enabling it. It seems logical to assume that if you accept that your sister undermines you or your boss doesn't give you support, or your kids won't listen, you will become a doormat if you're not upset about it. It seems reasonable to believe that if you accept that there's child abuse or animal cruelty or environmental devastation in the world, it means you've given up on the issue or just don't care.

But the opposite is true. Everything we do is infused with the energy and mindset with which we do it. As Mother Teresa said: "I was once asked why I don't participate in anti-war demonstrations. I said that I will never do that, but as soon as you have a pro-peace rally, I'll be there."[29]

---

[29] The Peace Alliance. Retrieved 2019. Peace & Inspirational Quotes. https://peacealliance. org/tools-education/peace-inspirational-quotes/

If we approach something we think is wrong in the world or in our lives with rage toward the thing that is causing the wrongness, we are creating more rage, not more peace in the world. When we see something that we believe needs to change, we can move toward a vision for that change without internal or external violence toward it. This is how we move forward. This is how we avoid the trap of trying to fight hate with hate, anger with anger, violence in the world with violence in our minds.

The only sane solution to any problem that creates suffering is to create peace. Peace is the only path that will lead to a final destination of more peace. Peace is the only way to repair something that is broken. And for many of us, our way of thinking about ourselves and our experiences has become broken. We know it's broken because it doesn't bring us any closer to the life we want: a life defined by creative and intentional use of our minds.

When we're stuck in what we don't want, it's time to change our mindset and to approach the situation at the level of the solution, not the level of the problem. To do this, we must first be willing to see things the way they really are. We accept them. Then we move forward with openness and clarity.

A Deeper Understanding

Take some time to process and integrate what you have learned in this section with some journal questions:

- How do you define success? How was this definition influenced by your parents or other important adults in your life? How was it influenced by your social group and society at large? How does this definition align with or deviate from your own values and vision for your life?

- How do you think your autonomic nervous system is primarily functioning at this time in your life? Are you in sympathetic or parasympathetic dominance? What signs or symptoms lead you to your conclusion?

- What is your take on the principle of feeling every feeling while questioning every thought? What challenges do you anticipate in experimenting with this idea?

- What are some of your most fear-based thoughts right now? How can you introduce more love and compassion, and therefore more peace to them?

- What are the most difficult feelings you are experiencing right now? How can you introduce more presence and acceptance to them?

- What are some ways you would like to experiment with creating more space between your thoughts, your feelings, and yourself?

- Where in your life have you been telling yourself that it's impossible to have peace? What can actually be changed in the here-and-now to experience more peace around this subject?

- What is your definition of acceptance? Did it change after reading the section on accepting and indifference? Did you find any opportunities for less suffering and greater peace for yourself in your own life?

Part 3: Create a Live You Love

How Do We Define Creativity?

What is creativity and how do we know when we have it? Is it a feeling? An action? A mindset?

How about all of the above?

Yet most of us don't consider creative living to be an integral part of life. In fact, creativity is something most of us don't think about very often, if at all. When life feels like it's being lived in a constant state of emergency, creative living can seem like a ridiculous proposition—the kind of thing that sounds nice in theory but completely impractical in reality.

Most of us can recognize the telltale signs of creativity's past presence: an oil-painted canvas, a beautiful outfit, a cleverly negotiated deal, a political movement, a dreamy photograph, a lavish garden, a cutting-edge invention, a hard-won connection. Creativity is not merely an act. It's certainly not merely a result. It's all of those things but also an energy, a mindset, a feeling, a connection to the sacred within each of us.[30]

Creative living is about surrender. It's about allowing ourselves to be led by something greater than the sum of our parts. Our creative nature is always in us, though it may lay dormant for years and even decades if we neglect it. Creativity is our natural state. It's written into our DNA by our ancestors and is infused in our feminine cycles. Yet we cannot meet with creativity unless we are open to receive it: mind, body, and soul.

The roots of creative thought grow most dependably in stillness, silence, and connection. We can never destroy our natural creative potential; we can only disconnect from it by blocking its flow through us. This happens when we become adrift in the fog of overwhelm, overwork, and overidentifying with external measures of success to define our internal sense of self.

The wisdom of our physical cycles can be a tool to deepen our connection to our creative energy. In both, we start with the fertile

---

[30] A fascinating article synthesizing research on the attributes of creativity and ideas for how to increase your own creativity: Gomez, J. 2017. What do we know about creativity? *The Journal of Effective Teaching.* 7(1): 31-43.

ground for a new idea. We then engage with the outside world to nurture and grow that idea until it becomes fully manifest and takes on a life of its own. Finally, we return inward and take stock of where our energy has been depleted and allow time and space for a renewal of our resources.

Neither creative nor physical cycles are about becoming something greater or better than ourselves. Instead, they're both a reflection of the depth of our participation with life. Through both we allow the divine wisdom already inside us to emerge and to make manifest the truths of our bodies and the wisdom of our souls. Both creative and physical cycles are conduits for participating in and coming to a greater understanding of the deeper world around us at increasingly powerful levels. Our secret lives, thoughts, dreams, and desires become our reality when we are in sync with the cyclical forces that drive creation itself.

The creative process happens most effortlessly when we are in a relaxed state—when we are in our parasympathetic nervous system. I have found that the degree to which a woman is living in perpetual fight-or-flight mode is the degree to which she has become disconnected from her own natural creative processes. This is because when the brain is filled with anxiety-driven neurochemicals, it cannot do the deeper, heart-centered processing that is required for creative thought. [31]

Another destroyer of creative energy for women is comparison. It is frighteningly easy to lose sight of what we actually want out of life. When we become overwhelmed with "shoulds," we lose our grip on our own desire, will, intuition, and presence. The need for external approval runs deep for most of us, and when we constantly feel we don't measure up, our uniqueness starts to be seen as the cause of our suffering instead of the path to our happiness.

The creative process requires us to let go of our attachment to outcome. When we create something new, we learn that while we may have given the object of our creation life, we cannot control the course its life takes once it is part of the world in its own right. In this understanding, we learn to let go of the illusion of control over the things we love most—the things that were once a part of us but now belong to themselves. We learn to love them for who and what they are, even if what they are isn't what we thought they would be.

---

[31] This article goes more in-depth about how creativity is hypothesized to work in the brain and why cortical arousal and stress inhibit remote associations required for creative thought: Heilman, K. 2016. Possible Brain Mechanisms of Creativity. *Archives of Clinical Neuropsychology*. 31 (4): 285-296. https://doi.org/10.1093/arclin/acw009

And so, the creative cycle becomes a teacher of a larger universal truth: that all creations are sovereign beings and their job is not to give us something we lack in ourselves. Their only job is to be there for us to love and enjoy.

It is the same way in our relationship with divine source energy that creates universes and people. We can have a relationship with the divine. We can even consider ourselves to be an aspect of the divine and to share many of its qualities. We can see the divine as being both outside and inside of us. But divine creative energy did not create us in order to validate itself or make itself feel like a legitimate creator or to get itself closer to perfection. It doesn't create to become anything. It creates because it is always seeking to be the most fully expressed version of itself.

Divine creative energy is already whole, perfect, and complete. Since it created us, that's how it sees us as well. We were created with free will to live our lives in a way that we believe would allow us to be the fullest, freest expression of ourselves. The creative energy doesn't dictate what we need to do or how we need to do it, but if we connect with it, it will give us all the support and guidance we need to exercise our free will and inner-wisdom in whatever ways that will most help us to learn and remember our own truths.

107

Creativity in all forms is about the joining of the stories of our own creation with who we are in the present moment and who we are yet to become. Engaging in the creative cycle changes us if we allow it to, but trust in the creative process is essential. We must decide that creative expression is there for our highest and greatest good and also accept that we're not supposed to understand how every step works or even what the next step is before we're ready to take it.

In this way, the creative process is a lot like walking through the forest in the middle of the night with only a flashlight. You will be able to see one or two steps in front of you and you will be able to tell if you're staying on the path, but you will not be able to see the whole path and you must trust that focusing only on each next right step will eventually get you to the other side safely.

This can be tricky for women who believe that everything they have that's good (relationships, career, money, etc) is because they have micromanaged every aspect of their lives up to this point. Trust and partnership with creative energy are essential to bringing into being what's in our imaginations and what's beyond it. It involves letting go: of our expectations, our addiction to control, and our belief that anything worth having must be acquired by force. It also involves holding on: to our intentions, our integrity, our sovereignty and our self-compassion.

Living With Intention

Creative living is all about harnessing the power of deliberate intention. An intention is a values-based direction that leads you on a meaningful path in your life. While intentions inform where you go in life and the choices you make, they are not end results. This is not unlike getting in your car and deciding to travel west. At what point have you traveled west? When you've been traveling for an hour? A week? When you reach the California coastline and can't drive any further without driving into the ocean? What if you decide to get in a boat and continue traveling? What if you travel so far west that you circle around the world and wind up back where you started?

The fact of the matter is, the minute your wheels started turning in a westerly direction, you were meeting your intention of going west. Intentions are a quality of what you choose to do with your life. They are not something that can ever be completed.

Creativity is the same way. You don't decide to be creative and then when you create something officially declare that you're now a creative person. The creative process is never done. It has no end. There is always more creative living to be had. This is because creative living is a direction, not an end result. It's a state of mind that understands there is always more to have, be, see, and do in life, and that the most powerful tool to create meaning in our lives is our mind.

Our creative works may bring good to the world and to our lives as expressions of our own inner-world made manifest for the external world, as a way to solve a problem in the world, or as a combination of the two.[32] Whatever our creative motivation, it is important that we approach our creative lives with the same openness, groundedness, and focus with which we live the rest of our lives.

If I decide to write a book about the harmful impact of plastic in our oceans and then in the middle I change my mind and decide that the best way to help solve this problem is to create a political movement on social media instead, I haven't stopped using my creativity to live my values, I've merely allowed my creativity to change form and become what it needs to in order to be the most fully expressed version of itself. My intention remains the same while the path to manifest that intention remains fluid.

---

[32] MacKinnon, D. W. 2005. IPAR's Contributions to the Conceptualization and Study of Creativity. Perspectives in Creativity. Taylor, I. A. & Getzels, J. W. (Eds.). Chicago, IL: Aldine Publishing Company.

It's easy to start a project with excitement and determination, only to veer off the path. Once off the path of intention, we risk chasing outside validation or completing projects we no longer feel aligned with for no other purpose than to be able to say we completed it. This is why it's so important to be clear on what the intention for the creative work is before we start and then on every step along the way.

We forget that it's not creativity's job to help us escape the areas in our lives that aren't working for us. We want our creative work to be responsible for our happiness or our confidence, to be responsible for our income, or to be our sole soul purpose. Yet when we do this, we outsource the responsibility of our feeling good onto something that is incapable of bearing that burden.[33]

Creativity is like anything else in life: it can only enhance the feelings we already have ourselves in our own lives. In this way, our relationship with creativity is much like any other relationship: we participate in it because it feels good for us to partner with the energy of another and create more good in our world and in the world in general. Our relationship with creativity also allows us to become aware of our own true nature. It can be a mirror that shows us how fully we are capable of

---

[33] More about how to have a healthy relationship with creativity in: Gilbert, E. 2015. *Big Magic: Creative Living Beyond Fear*. New York: Bloomsbury.

unconditionally loving something outside ourselves, which is in itself is a direct reflection of our ability to unconditionally love ourselves.

Creative intention is about getting clear on what you want and why you want it. Maybe it's a new career, freedom of time or money, a completed manuscript, a loving relationship, or political impact. Whatever it is, intention requires a vision for the future where good is manifested through you. Intention is the place where you and creative energy connect through purpose, imagination, and values. It's where you add to the treasure of the universe by creating your own.

The energy of intention is like a seed you plant in the ground. You may not know exactly what the seed will look like fully grown, but you do know the reason you're bothering to do the work in the first place. That reason doesn't have to be deep, ie: *I want to be a part of creation itself.* It could just be *I'd like to eat a fresh tomato this summer and planting this seed is the first step to get me there.* What matters is that the reason you're taking action to bring your creation into the world is clear and compelling to you.

The easiest way to get clear on your creative intention is to put it on paper. Spend some time with your journal brainstorming what you would like to have, be, see, or do in life, relationships, the world, and most importantly, in your mind. Plan how you will remain committed to your intention even when things get tough and the path forward becomes unclear. Ask yourself what will make the energy and dedication it requires "worth it" for you. Visualize yourself at the end of your creative journey with your finished product. What will it look like when it's complete? How will it feel? How will you know it's finished? Most importantly, how will the act of creation have changed you? How will it create more good in the world?

Getting clear on your *why* also helps you steer clear of buying into the fallacy that you need to create something in order to be someone. When we create something out of the belief that it will make us worthy, we put an unfair burden on our creation before we even start. It is the same as telling your creation: I'll allow you to exist only if you'll make me worthy by existing. This is a recipe for disaster.

A creation's "success" is subjective and fleeting at best. I have seen many women for whom creativity (whether it be artistic or problem-solving) and self-worth have become hopelessly intertwined. They are no longer creating because they love the act of creation. They are creating because they don't know who they are without the external accolades that come with a finished product. These women are no longer partners with their creative energy. They are now in a codependent relationship with it.

Creative living requires us to own our value. It gives us the opportunity to surprise and delight ourselves. Though your creative journey might leave you feeling in awe of our creative power, it shouldn't leave you with the belief that your accomplishments are in spite of yourself.

Intention allows you to make difficult decisions ahead of time so that you're not wasting your energy fighting yourself every step of the way. This is the foundation of discipline, which is an integral component of creative expression. If I decide to binge on Netflix or zone out on my phone instead of working on my book, I can rationalize that it's because I'm too tired or I don't have the energy to do what I value.

Ultimately though, I have to own that if I want the meaning, integrity, and fun that comes with creative living, I'm the only one who can determine it's worthy of my time and energy—no matter what. Intention helps me get to a place where I can not feel like doing something and still do it anyway because I know the net effect will be a better relationship with myself through the living out of my most deeply held values.

When Can I Call Myself a Creator?

When I had been trying for several months to get pregnant with my first child and realized that it wasn't happening right away like I wanted, I immediately started to wonder if it would ever happen. I wanted so badly to be able to call myself a mother, to hold a baby in my arms and know that she was mine, and yet that identity felt so far from where I was.

One day on the phone, almost a year into trying with still no pregnancy, I told my mom how helpless and uncertain I felt in the whole process and how horrible it was to want something so badly and to not be sure if I would ever have it.

"Just imagine that there's a baby out there for you and that it will come to you eventually when the time is right for it," my mom suggested.

That got me thinking: if there was a baby "out there" for me already, then that meant I was already it's mother. And if I was already it's mother and it was already my child, I could let go of my anxiety about it, and instead approach the situation like I imagined a mother would—with love and patience. I decided that from that day forward, I would stop focusing on being angry and frustrated that my baby wasn't arriving in the timeline I had arbitrarily decided was correct. Instead, I would focus on loving my child exactly as it was and exactly where it was until *she* decided that the time was right to come into existence and be with me.

Realizing that I already was a mother was a big relief. It meant I could relax and enjoy ALL parts of motherhood—even the part where I hadn't yet physically met my child and wasn't sure when I would. While the experience was still an extremely difficult one for me, my change in mindset offered great comfort.

The approach I used in taking on the identity of mother is the same approach I use in taking on the identity of a writer. I'm not waiting until my book is published to allow myself to believe I'm a legitimate writer. I call myself a writer now, and using that description allows me to see myself as one in my head and in my heart. This takes the pressure off creativity to give me something I don't feel I already have—like an identity. It puts the responsibility back on me to decide who I am and allows creativity to be there solely as my trusted friend on the journey.

Whether or not we ultimately share our creative works with the world is a personal decision. Putting yourself out there can feel scary and vulnerable. It always opens us up to the possibility that people might not like or see value in something we care deeply about. It's important to not get confused about our identities when our work is rejected or misunderstood by others.

It's important to remember that others see our work through their own eyes and relate to it based on their own past experiences and subconscious programming. It's nice to get acknowledgement for our efforts, and it hurts when we feel misunderstood or seen as not good enough. But in the end, the work cannot exist to validate us. We must decide that our work, as an honest expression of ourselves, is important and valid in its own right, just the same as us.

The Stories We Tell

Imagine you call a friend to chat but after a few minutes she cuts you off saying, "This actually isn't a good time to talk right now." Then she abruptly hangs up. You wait a few hours but she never gets back to you. You text her to see what's going on but get no response. Hours turn into days and you again try to check in but again get no response. You find yourself checking her social media several times a day to see what she's up to and then when you see a post about a "lazy Sunday," you tell yourself the story that she clearly has plenty of time to call you back and she's always been self-centered person and a lackluster friend and this incident proves it.

You tell yourself more stories to try to make sense of your friend's behavior and the thing they all have in common that you're the victim and she's the guilty one. You call other friends to get their opinions (really wanting them to commiserate with you about how wrongly you've been treated). You talk to your sister about what a crappy person your friend has turned out to be and she agrees. Finally, having enough evidence in your mind to convict her of having now and always been a terrible friend and a terrible person, you decide you're "done" with her. In reality, this means you declare you're cutting her out of your life while still continuing to fume over the situation on a daily basis

The net result of all this fear-based storytelling is that you feel hurt and rejected and you also no longer have that person as a friend. Stories you've been telling yourself your whole life, like "people suck" and "everyone disappoints me eventually" have gotten reinforced and re-lived. In your own mind, these stories are "right" and the more you tell them, the more you believe in their truth. Yet they also create and rein-force a feeling of victimhood you've been trying to escape since child-hood and ultimately lead to the ending of a once important friendship.

In this situation, telling a different story could have created a very different result—if not in the ultimate outcome, at least in your mind. What if instead of jumping right into telling yourself the story of what a self-centered person your friend is, you first acknowledged that you felt confused and wounded by her actions? Getting clear on your feel-ings before jumping to a fear-based conclusion allows you to remain present and take action based in clarity.

You send your friend an email telling her your feelings and also of-fering that you know there must be something going on because what she's doing is out of character for her. You let her know that you are always here for her but you also respect that she might need space for the moment. You don't look to others to reinforce that you are the victim in this situation. You instead use your creative energy develop some compassionate explanations for why someone like your friend would act this way.

This allows you to open your mind up to stories that don't have the effect of making you feel like a victim while cutting you off from your friend. Maybe you inadvertently did or said something that she was upset by but she didn't know how to tell you. Maybe she's going through a painful experience she's not ready to talk about for reasons that have absolutely nothing to do with you. Maybe her phone isn't working properly and she never received the text.

Doing this exercise allows you to create a path to peace in this situation, regardless of the external circumstances or your friend's behavior. It allows you to let go of fear-based stories that would otherwise become your default truth and to stay in integrity with your higher self. You come to understand that you can't control how your friend acts, but you can control how you react and you can own your power as the creator of your reality.

So often women live lives that are directed entirely by the fear-based stories they tell themselves. It's easy to create self-fulfilling prophecies without realizing it and these stories can wind up influencing every aspect of our lives. In all this, we lose power, creative drive, and most importantly, we lose ourselves.

Our stories are powerful creators of our reality, and yet their only source of power lies in our unquestioning belief in their truth. Owning our creative power is about the telling of a different kind of story—a story that honors our own truth and also makes us more of who we are, not less. Being known is a primal need, one deeply connected to both love and survival. When we tell our truth, we become known in all our perfect imperfection to ourselves and to the world.

The way we tell our stories allows us to determine whether we are the heroine or the victim of the events in our lives. Our story's power comes not from our circumstances, but from the way we choose to integrate and interpret them. We always have the power to move from the belief that our circumstances are happening *to* us to the belief that our circumstances are happening *for* us to learn, to grow, and to heal.

When we learn how to heal our own wounds through our power to create a different perception of reality for ourselves, we learn that the source of our most profound healing is within us all the time. Our own healing empowers us to share our stories with the world — not because we need the world's approval, but because we know the world needs us: our honesty, our rawness, and our truth-telling.

How We Silence Ourselves

"I'm just barely hanging on here. Taking time out of my day to do something I don't absolutely have to do is kind of way outside my scope right now. "

"I barely have time to take a shower. I don't have the energy for anything that's not a necessity."

"I'm just trying to get through the day. I'd love to do something to share my story, but it's not really that important to me."

Many of my clients work long hours and/or they have kids that demand a lot of time and energy. I get it. Deciding to take on a creative project in the midst of the daily chaos of your life can feel about as logical as deciding to organize your closet while your house is burning to the ground. But your creative work isn't the closet in a house that's on fire. It's the fire truck, the hose, the water, the homeowners insurance that brings with it the promise of support and renewal.

Many of us have been told throughout our lives that we are both too much and not enough. We buy into the story that we're not smart enough, creative enough, or important enough to add good to the world. Or that we're too scattered, unfocused, or ordinary to contribute anything of value. For most of us, our busyness can serve as protection from vulnerability and potential rejection. Yet it also confirms our belief in scarcity and reinforces a lack of balance in our lives.

Why try, we ask ourselves. It's this mindset that keeps us stuck where we don't want to be.

I've been there often myself. When my kids were younger and I was working full-time at a hospital, the idea of starting a creative project seemed laughable. But I did, and that project became my private practice, which now not only supports me, but serves as a conduit for my writing and other creative work, and allows me to provide life-changing value to every woman who walks through my door.

Yet I still from time to time find myself struggling with the story that my creative work is just not worth it. I convince myself that it's useless to put a lot of time and energy into something that may never see the light of day. I'd rather relax after the kids are in bed. I'd rather sleep in the morning. I'd rather surf the web on my free time. All those things have an immediate reward. They feel good in the moment. And if that's where it ended, there would really be no problem. But it's not. Because when we do something that's pleasurable in the moment but costs us our energy in the long-run, we compromise our own integrity and that never feels good.

Instead of telling myself the story that my efforts in writing this book will only be "worth it" if it changes the lives of millions of women, I can decide that it's irrelevant whether this book becomes a bestseller or is read by no one but my mom. In teaching this information to my imagined audience, I'm teaching it more deeply to myself. I become both the teacher and the student in this book, and so every time I sit down to write, I win, regardless of its external "success."

Of course, there are still times I decide that I don't want to write and so I give myself a break. I also don't try to force myself to be creative when what I really need to do is shut my mind off for a little while. I do, however, endeavor to consistently tell myself that my ideas are important and of value, that I have good to offer the world, and that I respect myself enough to keep my creative work as a priority in my life. Writing this book is a way to love and honor myself, and by extension, anyone else who may read it.

Ultimately, permission to prioritize something that has no real measurable goal and no guarantee of success is yours to give and yours to take. Decide that speaking your truth is a non-negotiable part of creating a life you love. Decide that being authentic in how you express yourself and live your life regardless of your external circumstances and responsibilities is important because you're important.

The tricky part is that this isn't a decision you need to make once. It's easy to decide that you're finally going to make yourself a priority, but what happens when you start a new job and need to put in long hours to prove yourself to your new team? What happens when your kid needs new hockey gear and you find yourself obliged to research what brand is both safest and cheapest? How about when your spouse or partner is stressed and you feel bad about not doing more to help out around the house? Surely during these times, it's okay to not prioritize creative work. It's only for an hour or a day or a few months.

The fact of the matter is, there may be times that life gets in the way and that you find you have other priorities than your creative work. And that's okay—as long as it's done with values-based intention. Conscious decision making is a part of life. The problem comes when we make assumptions about our obligations or when we decide from a place of fear.

If you feel like you really can't say no to any of your obligations and that won't change anytime in the foreseeable future, it may be time to take a look at that story. Who in your life has control over you and your time and energy? Is it you or someone else? Who or what is keeping you stuck? How and when did you lose choice in the matter of how your life is lived?

I've seen countless women in my private practice who can't consistently find ten minutes in their day for themselves. For them, it's hard to imagine a life where they choose to spend at least some of their time each week doing things that don't have a concrete, measurable outcome. They don't want to disappoint others. They believe no one can do what they do but them. They are terrified that if they let go of control, not only will they lose everything, they will also hurt the people they love most in the process.

It's ironic that the stories women tell themselves are the greatest impediment to telling their stories to the world. We blame society, our jobs, our families, our lack of talent for keeping us silent when really it's ourselves. It's our beliefs. Don't be a co-conspirator in the creation of your own mental prison. Love yourself enough to commit to being a creative person every day. Whether it's for five minutes or five hours is less important than simply giving yourself a consistent experience. And when you do, the loving, creative energy of the universe can't help but co-create with you.

How to Begin

There are three essential elements for harnessing your creative voice:

1. Listen.
2. Trust.
3. Let go.

Creativity is an energy—a force we partner with. It's is not an event or an outcome we need to *make* happen. We only need to *allow* the energy to flow through us and remove the blocks to access what's already there. While every creative manifestation will be unique, the structure for how it unfolds tends to stay the same. Creative expression requires that we get clear on our purpose, that we silence our minds and open our hearts, and that we take our attachment to the end result out of the picture.

Let's look at each of these elements more closely.

Listen

Our minds are a veritable firehose of thoughts, feelings, and information but creativity requires presence. This means we need to turn off the fire hose and instead dip our bucket into the well of intuition and inner-wisdom we all have inside of us.[34] Still, it would be difficult to shut off our minds entirely, and even if we could, we wouldn't want to. Our minds are where our personalities lay. They're the place where everything that makes us human exists. The mind is a part of who we are, and as we discussed before, it's an important part. We just don't want its noise and urgency to drown out the still, small voice within us.

One of the easiest tools I've found to clearly connect with my own inner-wisdom is to directly ask it questions in my journal. I find that when I do this, I always get clarity I would never get if I was just trying to think my way to understanding a situation.

This involves sitting quietly and writing a question about the problem as I understand it in my mind. I then wait for an answer to come through me and onto the paper.

---

[34] An in-depth article with research on intuition, what it is and isn't and the difference between intuition and intuitive judgment: Dörfler, V., and F. Ackerman. (2012). Understanding intuition: The case for two forms of intuition. *Management Learning*. 43(5): 545-564. sagepub.co.uk/journalsPermissions.nav DOI: 10.1177/1350507611434686

Here is an example:

* * *

I'm feeling really overwhelmed today. What do I need to know to feel and give love to the world instead of fear today?

Be open to receiving it.

How do I do that?

Create all experiences with intention.
Put forth love for its own sake, not to answer fear.
Trust that love is all powerful, all knowing, and always enough.
Trust in your own power to give deeply from an infinite well.
Trust love to take care of you.
Work from your heart, not your mind.
Let go of distraction.
Feel love's power working though you and in you.
Be present and notice love's presence in all you do today.

That all sounds great, but I don't feel like I have enough time to do everything I need to do each day. And also, I don't feel I have enough focus for all of that.

Plan your time with intention. Don't leave time to be figured out in the moment. You can actually make time—create it—by deciding ahead of time how it will be spent. Much of your time is lost in the in-between of your day. You don't know what to do next so you do nothing. You don't plan because you're afraid.

What am I afraid of?

That you will plan and you will fail to follow the plan. That you will disappoint yourself. You have a story that you are a terrible planner and your reality reflects that story. Making a plan and following that plan is a part of your self-relationship. You have always believed that you are flawed in this way. To be clear, planning does not give you value. That is where you are confused. You believe it does and you believe you are less valuable because you don't plan. Planning is neither good nor bad. It's just something you do. Planning is something that you feel good doing, and that is the reason to do it. That is really the only reason to do anything.

I guess I never thought of that piece before—that I decide to plan, then I don't follow through on that plan and I believe I'm a lesser person because of it. I guess planning can just be a tool I choose to use because it enhances my life and gives me clarity, not because it gives me value or helps me achieve things that give me value.

This is what I mean when I say be open to receiving love. *I mean always and in all ways. Even when it comes to planning.*

I got it. Thank you and I love you.

I love you too, Amy.

* * *

I am constantly getting wisdom and answers to questions I have about my life with this method. The inner-wisdom within me is, frankly, a whole lot wiser that I am.

What does your inner-wise woman have to say to you? Try getting out your journal and asking it a question about a problem you're having right now. You might be surprised by what you hear when you listen through your pen.

Before we create anything in our lives, especially something we're unsure about, it is important that we listen first. When we experience uncertainty or confusion about something, it usually means we don't have enough information. Or rather, the human in us doesn't have enough information. Our intuition in us always knows the way. We just need to ask and be open to hearing the answer.

Trust

Creating what you want in your life requires a strong, trusting relationship with yourself. Pursuing a creative dream requires integrity and self-respect. These qualities are what enable us to stick to a commitment even when it seems difficult. They're what drives us to keep going even when it's hard or it seems pointless. To trust yourself means to believe in your own truth, ability, and strength.

Trust also comes into play when you don't know the next right step. When you're stuck in a place of not knowing where to go or even what you really want, can you trust then that you have everything within you to find the answers you need?

Ultimately, creativity is about both giving and receiving. We *receive* inspiration from universal creative intelligence, we take inspired action, and then we *give* our creation a life of its own by sharing it once again with the universe. As you begin, go into it with the expectation that it will feel difficult, uncomfortable, and frustrating—especially in the beginning. But trust that it will ultimately, unquestionably, be worth it.

Let Go

It will be very difficult to begin if you're afraid to fail. In order to be successful, we must take failure out of our vernacular. The fact is we learn by doing. When we "fail," we learn. Then we try again and either achieve the desired result or learn more and fail better. The fun and joy of the process aren't in the end result. They're in the doing, the learning, the discovering we do along the way.

It can be a relief to realize that failure is not a threat to us at all. Failure is nothing more than a story we buy into with the net result that it keeps us trapped in the experience of being stuck. To get past the inevitable feeling of panic we all experience when we go outside our comfort zone, we have to let go of our stories about failure and realize that in the creative process, there is only learning and winning.

Whenever a woman creates something, there comes a time when that creation becomes ready to take on a life of its own. Letting go is about loving our creation enough to trust that it is capable of standing on its own in the world. It means understanding that our creation can only thrive when we're not micromanaging all aspects of it and that when we allow our creation to move and flow freely, it becomes exactly what it was always meant to be: itself.

Our creative cycles mirror every other cycle in nature: there is a time for holding our energy close, nurturing it deeply and shielding it from the stresses of the outside world. Then there is a time when that energy benefits from interacting with the outside world. This interaction helps our creation to go from theoretical to real and to take on a consciousness of its own.

For this to happen there is another thing we need to let go of, and that's the notion of "perfect." We've all heard that perfect is the enemy of good, but perfect is also the enemy of good enough. It's the enemy of presence. It's the enemy of conscious creation. Creativity's only obligation to us is to give us the experience of itself. Whether what you create is objectively perfect—or even good—is irrelevant.

Stop telling yourself you don't have any original ideas or that you're terrible at what you do or that you're not worth it. Creative living is always worth it because you're always worth it. You are of the energy of the divine. Your story is sacred. You contain within you the same creative force that builds worlds, galaxies, universes. Open yourself to that energy while letting go of the outcome, and you have begun the first step on a never ending journey home to yourself.

Getting Support

I am amazed by the number of women I meet who wouldn't think twice about sitting through hours of their kids' travel soccer games or waking up at 3 A.M. to take a conference call in Asia or going to a friend's party even though they are exhausted and just want to go to bed. Yet the idea of blocking off a few hours of the week for themselves sounds laughable to them. It's like our ability to take action goes into overdrive when it serves another person, but becomes completely paralyzed when it comes to ourselves.

I highly recommend tracking and recording your time for two weeks to see how much time you spend doing what others want you to do (or what you believe you *should* be doing) and how much time you spend doing things for no other purpose than it feels good to you.[35] Like many women, you may be shocked to find that you

---

[35] You can do this by filling out a spreadsheet with the hours of each day of the week divided into 15 or 30 minute increments or by setting a reminder to record the information in a notebook or on your phone throughout the day. Be as detailed as possible to get as clear an understanding as you can of where your time is *actually* spent vs where you believe it's being spent. I strongly encourage you to do this exercise, as the insights it can give you about your life are invaluable.

can't identify a single hour in the week where you intentionally put yourself first.

I say intentionally because flopping on the couch in exhaustion and watching TV while you scroll through social media doesn't count. Doing the basics like taking a shower or sitting down to eat a meal doesn't count either. I'm talking about blocking off time in your schedule ahead of time, saying "no" to anything that conflicts with your commitment to yourself, and then sticking to that commitment when the scheduled time comes—no matter who or what else might be demanding your attention.

Note: obviously if your baby is screaming and no one else is home or if you're actually supposed to be doing something else—like your job— it's not a good time to be starting a creative or self-care activity. The point here is not to not do the things you took responsibility to do. That would *not* help us to live more according to our values-based inten- tions. The point is to create a balance where your energy isn't always going outward to serve other people, but is consciously being turned inward on a regular basis in order to serve your highest self.

We need to stop seeing saying "yes" to the demands of the world as being virtuous while seeing saying "yes" to ourselves as selfish. Ultimately, no one can give us the permission to create a life we love but ourselves. That being said, we need to surround ourselves with those who support our creativity or it will always be an uphill battle.

My husband, also a writer, and I have an agreement—we can always take time for our creative works, no questions asked from the other person. I know how important his writing is to him. It's an integral part of who he is. Therefore, I see not getting annoyed that I have to take the kids by myself for a couple of hours as a way to express my love and respect for who he is as a person, and I know he sees it the same way.

We both make it a point to frequently encourage each other's creativity, to take an interest in each other's projects, and to be each other's cheerleader. I have also come to see my husband as a mentor in how to add more integrity to my own creative work. He has shown me what dedication, focus, practice, and patience look like as someone who honors his own creativity and sees it as an important and worthy use of his time.

Maybe it's because he has not been socialized to take care of everyone but himself. Maybe it just comes naturally to him. Either way, the fact that doing things that support him to be his best self also benefits those around him is obvious. This fact hasn't always been obvious to me though so I use him as a model for how to set my own boundaries around my work and to honor it as important and valuable.

It hasn't always been this way though. There was once a time when I resented my husband for taking time for himself and didn't feel he was very good at expressing support for me. In fact, I felt like no one supported me. Getting to this point in my relationship has required a lot of mindset work on my part and honest, non-defensive communication on both our parts. In order to have the experience of feeling supported, I needed to first look at the ways I wasn't supporting myself and also wasn't supporting the people I was expecting support from.[36]

If you are feeling unsupported in your life, I invite you to look at the ways you're not supporting yourself first. Explore the ways you can provide more support to yourself and how you can meet your own needs. Next look at the ways in which open and honest communication with those you want support from is possible. Use your creative problem solving power and tools of self-expression to think about how to communicate in ways that others can hear you. Let them know what

[36] The book *The Mastery of Love* by Don Miguel Ruiz was invaluable to me in learning what it means to be in a loving relationship and *how* to be in a loving relationship. Other great books on creating a loving, supportive relationship are *Getting the Love You Want* by Harville Hendrix, *The Seven Principles of Making Marriage Work* by John Gottman, and *The Five Love Languages* by Gary Chapman.

would be helpful to you in a loving, non-accusatory way and then be willing to let go of your attachment to the outcome.

I understand that this might be easier said than done because if you're like most women, you have had experience with toxic or dysfunctional relationships or environments in your life. Who among us can say she has never been hurt, abused, rejected, bullied, assaulted, misunderstood, made to feel small, insulted, slandered, manipulated or victimized?

If you're in a situation where you feel that way now, it is imperative that you get out. I understand that might not be physically possible right away, but the mindset of resignation, of having no options needs to change immediately.

While support for anything we do in life ultimately needs to begin from within, we also need to surround ourselves with family, friends, and teachers who believe in us, are about what we're about, and who love us for who we already are—not who they're hoping we'll someday become.

Introvert or extrovert, women are designed to be relational in nature. We thrive when we receive support from our own loving tribe and when we feel that we are able to support and add value to them in turn, particularly during periods of stress.[37] We don't want people in our lives who reinforce our own negative thinking that life sucks and there's nothing we can do about it. We don't want a support system that consists entirely of people who validate our self-defeating behavior while they continue to engage in their own. We want to surround ourselves with people who will both move and ground us.

The process to finding or deepening these relationships is the same as you will use in any other creative process: set an intention, create a vision, take focused action, protect your boundaries, renew, and repeat. If you have no one in your life to serve as a creative mentor for you, you may try using the internet to find and study those who have come from where you've come from and are now where you want to be. Develop a friendship with them in your mind—even if you never actually speak to them. Learn about their mindset, how they show up in the world, and their creative process in all they do.

Ask yourself what aspects of this person you most appreciate and look for examples of how those aspects may be present in you and in your life (even if it's in a much more general way.) The beauty of the world-

---

[37] The biobehavioral causes of female tendency to "tend and befriend," particularly in times of stress, is discussed at length in this article: Taylor, S., L. C. Klein, B. Lewis, T. Gruenwald, R. Gurung, J. Updegraff. (2000). Biobehavioral response to stress in females: Tend-and befriend, not fight-or-flight. *Psychological Review.* 107(3):411-429.

wide web is that we have access to knowledge and people we never would in our regular lives.

Understanding what is possible by witnessing it in others is a gift beyond measure. When we create relationships with supportive people (whether in real life or in our imaginations), we begin to understand what the world has to offer to us. And what it has to offer is everything.

Creating Something Better

A bby was stuck in a toxic work environment. Her boss was demanding and controlling and encouraged competition between Abby and her team members. Abby was constantly terrified that her job was in jeopardy—something that caused her great anxiety, as she had just purchased her first apartment and had little savings to fall back on if she lost her job. She began to have panic attacks several times per week and had trouble sleeping at night, which only added to her stress.

Feeling more and more stuck, the situation started to feel overwhelming to Abby. She couldn't find the motivation to seriously look for another job because she was so burnt-out at the end of each day. She spent much of her time at home on her couch binge-watching TV while she scrolled social media. There, she compared herself to other women who seemed to be living happy and carefree lives in all of their pictures and she wondered what she was doing wrong.

When Abby tried to discuss her situation with friends, they responded by complaining about their own career situations. "You think that's bad..." seemed to be the theme of every conversation.

In our work together, Abby began to explore and understand the dynamics of her relationships with both her coworkers and her friends. She had grown up in a family where complaining about life was the way to connect with others. Hard work was assumed to be the cost of both success and self-worth. If something were to be achieved, it would have to mean pain and sacrifice would take place to get there.

The unspoken message Abby received was that if things came easily to her, it would mean she had nothing in common with those she loved most. Abby had unconsciously carried this dysfunctional way of relating to others into adulthood where the competitive environment at work and the negative attitude of her friends only served to reinforce the belief that suffering was a requisite to having the things she wanted and needed in life.

Determined to change this pattern, Abby decided to consciously address some of the negative beliefs that had led her to being stuck in a toxic job situation. In doing this, she was able to put an action plan into place. She remembered that she had a supportive colleague a few years back and reached out to her to help her explore how to best navigate her work situation. The former colleague was delighted to hear from Abby and mentor her on how to break into job opportunities that would use Abby's skills in ways she had never considered before.

Abby decided to stop discussing her work situation with her friends and family entirely and instead explore opportunities to meet new people from different backgrounds and with different views on life, though it was still a challenge to separate herself from this long-standing mindset. She began to internalize that her self-worth didn't need to come from struggle or hustle.

One day while on her way home from work, Abby passed a local yoga studio that offered a yoga teacher training. The studio had always been there, she had just never noticed it because in the past, she had been too burnt out on her commute to notice much of anything. Abby had done yoga on and off for years and loved the idea of becoming a teacher, but immediately dismissed it because it would be too time consuming and wouldn't be financially lucrative. Ultimately, however, she decided to try it, reasoning that even if teaching yoga never became her main profession, she was still interested in learning as much as she could about it for its own sake.

This decision was way outside her comfort zone because it required her to spend money and energy on something that wasn't necessary or part of a larger plan for objective success. Still, Abby decided that investing in her passion was worthy in its own right. Doing so allowed her to see herself as a whole person who was willing to honor her own creative expansion without worrying about whether it will lead to external success or approval.

While the yoga teacher training gave her a lifelong understanding of yoga philosophy and practice, and ultimately opened up the doors to a side gig teaching yoga at an assisted living, the most profound gift it gave her was a community of like-minded people who were fabulously supportive. It was an invitation to a world where she was finally able to understand competition as an optional mindset, not a prison.

Abby created not just a new mindset but a new reality for herself and this is something we can all do. It only requires that we are uncompromising in our willingness to honor our true nature.

The Creative Mindset

There are two universal truths that we must maintain awareness of if we want to experience our unique creative nature:

1. Everything is created twice: first in our minds and then in our external experience.
2. The highest creative expression and the innermost creative expression are one.

We need to be able to visualize and emotionally step into the identity of the woman who has created before we can physically experience it. It's important to see in our mind's eye the result we are aiming for and even more important to feel as if it's already happened.

I have had clients ask me what the point of trying to achieve something is if they already feel as though they have it. What motivation would they have for doing the work to make it happen if they already have the feeling they thought it would bring?

I respond that engaging in creative work doesn't make us something we previously were not. It reveals who we already are. I became a mother when I acknowledged that a mother was who I already was, not when the world gave me proof of it's truth and permission to believe it. I became a book writer the minute I decided to write the book, not only if it becomes a best-seller or receives critical acclaim.

Why bother to write a book if I can just pretend I'm a writer now and save myself the work? Because calling myself a writer and then never writing would not feel congruent. I don't just want the title of writer—I want the experience that goes with it.

There is a difference between pretending to be something I know I'm not and embracing who I am and then becoming even more of it. On the other hand, feeling like I'm a book writer and then actually engaging in the act of writing a book feels completely congruent because it makes the highest expression and the innermost expression one. In other words, deciding that I'm already a book writer feels good. Engaging in the act of writing the book without having to struggle with beliefs like *I need to finish this book so I can become a real author or a legitimate writer* also feels good. Both give me the complete experience of creation.

Authors write things. Painters paint things. Scientists study things. Spouses and partners love. Leaders lead. Teachers teach. We so often make it so much more complex than that. We decide that we can only call ourselves a teacher if we're being paid full-time to stand in front of a classroom of students. We forget that we can teach people all day every day both directly and indirectly through our words, our actions, and our deeds.

Likewise, I was a therapist long before I got my master's degree and started getting paid to change lives for a living. I have always felt I was a therapist, and so I always have been (although that doesn't mean I was always licensed in an official capacity to do so). What being a therapist has looked like for me has been a creative evolution. My skills have grown and been refined over the years. My interests have changed. My knowledge has expanded. And so while I had to start out seeing the truth in the statement "I'm a therapist" from the beginning, my understanding of that truth has deepened and will continue to deepen throughout my entire career and after.

Just as we discussed earlier with the power of intention and the metaphor of traveling west, the minute I point my identity toward being something I want to be, I'm already there. But the more I travel in the direction of that identity, the more there is to see, feel, do, and know

153

about it. Even better, the more I get to discover about myself as a person in the context of that identity, which is *so* much fun.

Part of creating something is coming to the realization that it already exists. Whether it exists in the world is far less important than embracing its existence in our minds. This can be a difficult concept to wrap our minds around. We tend to believe something exists only when we see it or at least see evidence of it, but in order to see it, we have to believe it first.

How does this work? By noticing where the thing you want to create is already true and then finding ways to make it more true both in your mind and in physical reality. In order to have love, we must be loving. In order to have freedom, we must exercise our own free will. In order to have the experience of being a creator, we must notice what we have already created in our lives. In order to live in a peaceful world, we must live with peace in our hearts.

It is a mistake to create things in our lives because of how we believe they will make us feel. The journey must be congruent with the destination. So if you want to be happy, and you decide that being a successful photographer will make you happy, and then you kill yourself trying to create that success, you will have destroyed the very thing you set out to have in the first place.

If, on the other hand, you can decide you want to be happy and there-fore decide you *are* happy regardless of your external circumstances, then nothing outside yourself needs to take on the responsibility of making you happy. If you then decide that photography enhances the happiness you already have and so you spend time doing photography and consider yourself to be a photographer, then you're not only a suc-cess, you're also happy—even if no one ever sees your pictures.

That being said, the act of creation can naturally bring with it negative feelings and those negative feelings can cause us to question our cre-ative journey. Sometimes creativity stops feeling good in the moment and we are faced with the decision of whether to move forward into uncertainty where frustration and failure threaten to overtake us. You see your TV beckoning with Netflix and a comfy couch. Your phone is sitting right there on the table full of emails and Instagram stories for you to lose yourself in. There is a bottle of wine and a glass on the counter and drinking enough to soften all the hard edges of life sounds much more appealing than trying to focus on a project that you may never even finish.

When this happens, you can always return to your intention. Why did you decide to embark on this journey in the first place? What are you telling yourself about yourself if you abandon your intention when it feels hard or confusing? There is sometimes a difference between feeling pleasure in the moment and feeling happy in a bigger sense. Living in integrity, even when it's hard, has the net effect of supporting the development of our dignity and inner-peace. The more you live in integrity with your intentions and values, the more you will learn to trust yourself.

Most of us are terrible at starting new things. Beginnings are scary. They put us outside our comfort zone, where our sympathetic nervous system hates to be. It is painful to struggle with something, the way we often do at the beginning, and to not have a guarantee that it will be "worth it." Most of us are also terrible at persevering. We naturally lose energy and interest in our long-term projects, whether it's deciding to get healthy, starting a podcast, finishing a degree, or fighting for a cause, it's easy to lose steam when things get difficult or overwhelming.

Mentally rehearsing and visualizing yourself following through on your intention, having discipline, and acting according to your values, even when things are difficult can help you have a positive outcome.[38] For example, if I mentally rehearse going to an all-you-can-eat sushi

---

[38] A study on how this process works: Frank, C., W. Land, C. Popp, T. Schack. 2014. Mental representation and mental practice: Experimental investigation on the functional links between motor memory and motor imagery. *PLoS One.* Frank C, Land WM, Popp C, Schack T. Mental representation and mental practice: experimental investigation on the functional links between motor memory and motor imagery. *PLoS One.*;9(4):e95175. Published 2014 Apr 17. doi:10.1371/journal.pone.0095175

place and only eating to the point of being satisfied, not painfully full, the chances that that will happen when I'm actually in the restaurant will go up significantly. Likewise, if I visualize myself getting out of bed at 5:15 and working on my book for an hour even if I'm tired or my warm and cozy bed is calling to me, it is much more likely my book will get done.

There are also times when taking a break is an important and necessary part of the process. How do we know the difference? We go inward and find clarity. We allow this part to take as long as it needs and we don't impose fear on it by worrying that we've lost our passion or we're stuck or we're going to fail if we don't force ourselves to keep moving forward. We trust: in ourselves, in our vision, in the cyclicality of the creative process. We take time for renewal with intention.

There is a delicate balance that women must negotiate on the creative path. This balance can only be achieved by connecting with our own intuition and inner-wisdom. Doing this requires outer and inner work. The outer work looks like taking action with intention and vision. The inner-work looks like getting still and quiet, listening to our intuition, and getting aligned with our values and purpose.

Creation honors and celebrates our uniqueness because it involves bringing forth into existence something that didn't exist before and could only exist through us. If we create from a place of love for the thing we're creating, we automatically bring an increase of good to the world. And reciprocally, any time we increase the world's good, we remember our own as well.

Opening Up

Before moving on to the next chapter, take some time with your journal to reflect on creativity's presence in your life.

- How does creativity show up in your life?
- What is your creative work? How has that work changed at different points in your life?
- What are some ways your creative voice has been silenced by others? What about yourself?
- What are some "shoulds" you need to let go of in order to make more space for creativity in your life?
- What is a big creative project you have always wanted to do? What has stopped you in the past? What would need to change in the future for you to see this project complete?
- What are some ways you can integrate creativity into your everyday life? How would your life change if you did some of these things on a regular basis?
- Have you ever shared a creative work with the world and gotten a negative response? How did that response color your view of yourself? Of your creative ability? Of the world?

- What stories do you tell yourself about your ability to create what you want in life? What is the origin of those stories? Would telling a different story have a different result? What story would you like to be true about your present and your future?

- Where in your life are you feeling stuck?

- What support do you need to be able to create a peaceful path in life? What people, places, or things need to change? What needs to stay the same?

- What role does mindset play in your creative life?

- What mindsets do you need to change before you can manifest your creative vision? Which do you need to deepen?

Part 4: Set Yourself Free

How to Stop and Smell the Roses

B y now, you might be thinking of the peaceful path as a mighty, life-altering undertaking. You're right, but it's a path that begins with simple mindset shifts and actions that will have massive impact on how you experience your life. When we let go of trying to figure out our past and trying to control our future, we are left with only the present moment. All healing begins here, because after all, the present moment is really all we have. Everything else is nothing but a story we tell ourselves about what was or what will be.

There is one key tool I invite you to explore that can help you to find peace in the present moment: mindfulness. By exploring and regularly making a practice of mindfulness, we can begin to let go of the constant chatter in our brains, soften our hearts, and take ownership of our daily experiences of life.[39] These tools gift us with a newfound ability to experience each moment without judgment or inflamed thinking—regardless of what that moment brings.

---

[39] An article with just some of the myriad of research on the benefits of mindfulness: Brown, K. W., R. M. Ryan, and J. D. Creswell. 2007. Mindfulness: Theoretical foundations and evidence for its salutary effects. *Psychological Inquiry.* 104(27): 211-237.

Fear is not something we are born with. It's something we inherit by being born into a world where the absolute truth of love is questioned. The practice of mindfulness is the practice of returning to a state of love. This state is synonymous with our innermost being, but is also often described as joy, peace, health, appreciation, ease, relief, connection, or any of the other emotions that remind us of who we really are at a soul level.

Mind*less*ness begins as a way to cope with living in an overwhelming, increasingly fast paced, chaotic world, and quickly takes over our lives if we're not vigilant toward its presence.[40] In the modern world, it has become not only a habit but an addiction to check out of our lives every time we have an uncomfortable feeling.

Our brains are wired to respond positively to the acquiring of new information. In fact, every time we get a new piece of information, we get a little hit of dopamine—the neurotransmitter responsible for reward-motivated behavior.[41] This information-reward connection is a

---

[40] More about mindfulness vs. mindlessness and the negative consequences of mindlessness in our personal and professional lives can be found in this article: Epstein, R. M. 1999. Mindful practice. *Journal of the American Medical Association.* 282: 833-839.doi:10.1001/jama.282.9.833

[41] Taber, K. H., D. Black, L. J. Porrino, R. A. Hurley. 2012. Neuroanatomy of dopamine: Reward and addiction. *The Journal of Neuropsychiatry and Clinical Neurosciences.* Published online Jan 1, 2012. 24(1): https://doi.org/10.1176/appi.neuropsych.24.1.1

survival mechanism passed down to us from our primitive ancestors who lived in a world where life and death were contingent on getting information that was typically both slow and hard to come by.

Compare that with the information overload our brains now have to process on a daily basis: email, social media, texts, voice messages, and appointments on our phones. 24/7 news coverage with scared angry voices on all sides adding new commentary and opinions designed to incite outrage every few seconds. We also have access to movies, TV, books, games, music, and all manner of electronic devices to entertain us before, during, and after work, family time, and personal time.

The list goes on and on, but I'm sure you get the point. Where the days of our ancestors were filled with work, physical movement, pleasure, creativity, and connection, our days are filled with what is essentially mental fast food. Our brains have come to crave the constant flow of new information and soon we get to a place where we are filled with uncomfortable feelings any time we're forced to be silent and still for a few moments.

Mindfulness is a way to bring our lives back to the present moment, one moment at a time.[42] It is about being fully open, focused, and grounded with whatever life has to offer us without wanting it to be

---

[42] Carlson, C. E., J. A. Asten, and B. Freedman. 2006. Mechanisms of mindfulness. *Journal of Clinical Psychology.* 62(3): 373-386.

different. The point of mindfulness is not to intellectualize every experience so that it means nothing but rather to avoid responding purely out of fear or habit.

If we're experiencing something we truly enjoy—sitting on the beach on a gorgeous summer day, for example: we can enhance that experience and even expand and slow down our sense of time by focusing with greater specificity on what it is about our experience that we're enjoying: the feeling of warm sand between our toes, the gentle breeze on our bare skin, the salty smell of the air, the sight of the spectacular blues and greens of the ocean, the sparkle of the sun on the waves, the wonder at the connection between the oceans of the world, how it contains both the tiniest and largest forms of life...the list can go on and on. But when we're busy creating an Instagram story of our experience and then checking the feedback of our followers, we rob ourselves of the opportunity to experience deep connection to the best that life has to offer.

Conversely, mindfulness can also give us the experience of speeding up time when we are faced with an experience we judge as unwanted or unpleasant. For example, I love doing laundry but I hate hanging up my clothes. I do, however, love the experience of walking into my closet and seeing all of my clothing properly put away and hung up so I can easily choose what to wear for the day.

For years, I avoided hanging my clothes up because I just didn't like to do it. Freshly cleaned clothes would wind up sitting on a pile on a chair in my room, getting more and more wrinkly and I would stress in the morning digging through the pile to find a particular item buried within. Often, two or more loads would pile up, creating a mountain of clean clothing that would be the first thing I saw when I woke up in the morning and the last thing I saw before I went to bed.

Finally, I decided enough was enough and began to experiment with adding the practice of mindfulness to this dreaded task. I started to pull the laundry out of the dryer as soon as it was done so that I could experience that fresh laundry smell and feel the cozy warmth of the clothing in my hands. This was especially appealing in the winter months when I was in a constant state of feeling cold no matter what I was wearing.

I would take the clothing to my closet where I would appreciate each item for its beauty, noticing the different textures in my hands as I hung it up and appreciating how it made me feel when I wore it that week. If I had a lot to hang up at once, I would take a few seconds to put on some music I enjoyed or a podcast I was dying to finish. And when I was done, I made sure to take a moment to bask in the end result: the fact that I had a closet full of clothing to hang up in the first place, and the fact that I love how it looks and feels when everything I own is in its proper place instead of forgotten in a pile.

Doing this turned a task that felt painful and annoying into one that felt like a spiritual experience. The task had to get done one way or another, but my mindset of awareness and presence determined whether I experienced it as energy draining or energy giving.

Mindfulness brings us out of the burnout cycle and into the peace cycle and empowers us to decrease our experience of suffering in every area of life—large and small. Becoming and staying mindful isn't a one and done deal. It's a lifelong practice and process of letting go of the identity of powerlessness and passivity where we believe that life is happening to us, and instead cultivate an inner attitude of dignity, patience, self-acceptance, and self-reliance where we believe life is happening for us and through us.

Mindful Eating

One of the most basic ways to practice mindfulness as we go about our day is with our meals. The process of learning to eat mindfully is the process of learning to nurture ourselves with compassion and respect. When we cut out the distractions that happen when we eat while sitting in front of a screen, traveling, or engaging in any other type of mindless activity, we not only learn to eat with dignity, we also give ourselves the gift of being fully present to enjoy one of the most pleasurable activities we do.

Try this:

- Think about your favorite meal. Ask yourself: what food gives me the greatest pleasure while I'm eating it and has the net effect of feeling great when I'm done? For me, it's a piece of gluten-free toast topped with arugula, smashed avocado, fried egg, sea salt, and salsa.

- Prepare your meal with positive anticipation for the experience you're about to have.

- Sit down at a table with no distractions—no phone, no laptop, no book, no work. It should be just you and your food.

- Before you begin eating, set an intention to be fully present with your meal, to enjoy each bite, and to stop when you experience fullness. Decide to eat with complete respect not only for the food you're about to consume but also for yourself. Take a moment of gratitude for the sun, water, and soil, plants, animals, and people that came together to bring to you the food you're about to consume. Allow for a moment of wonder as you think about all the systems that needed to be in place for the food to make its way to your plate.

- As you take your first bite, notice the flavor as it hits your tastebuds. Experience the different textures in your mouth. For my avocado toast, I notice the smooth creaminess of the avocado first, then the crispy crunch of the toast, the tang of salt, the bitterness of the arugula, and the spice of the salsa. The unique combination creates a delightful experience for my senses.

- Put your hands down and allow yourself to fully chew your food until it is completely broken down in your mouth before swallowing.

- Pause to breathe before taking the next bite.

- Continue this way until you feel satisfied; then stop. You will probably find it to be a lot easier than it might otherwise be to be in-tune with your satiation point because you're present with your physical and emotional sensations throughout the entire experience.

- When you're done, notice the difference between this experience and your normal experience of eating a meal. What aspects of it were enjoyable? What aspects were tricky?

It's normal to find yourself having several experiences at once. There were likely moments of experiencing deep pleasure and peace in the act of slowing down and mindfully eating a meal. At the same time, you might have found yourself feeling bored, antsy, anxious, or even angry at mono-tasking when you're used to multitasking. It's also very likely your mind wandered many times, forgetting the original intention of presence and instead focusing on trying to manage the past or the future with your thoughts.

By eating mindfully, we become aware of what has been available to us all along—nourishment, a sense of fullness of life, and a sense of loving gratitude. We stop using food as yet another way to avoid feeling uncomfortable feelings. Instead, we begin to understand that there is no feeling we can't handle and that every feeling can be welcome without judgment, because all feelings are temporary and all feelings are human.

Our compulsive drive to multitask every aspect of our lives is, in effect, a refusal to fully live. How can we say we're alive and yet not be aware of the most basic of human experiences as we're having them? The act of doing something and the awareness of actually doing it are two very different things. It's quite possible to be both present and absent as one meal turns into one day turns into one year turns into one lifetime. Mindful eating is a way to reclaim our awareness, our sovereignty, our peace—to stop being passive spectators in our lives and start being wholehearted participants.[43]

---

[43] Another helpful mindful eating exercise can be found in this article: Nelson JB.2017. Mindful Eating: The Art of Presence While You Eat. *Diabetes Spectr.*30(3):171-174.

The Four-Way Stop

W omen tend to be very stuck in their heads, and so for most of us, this is where life takes place. We will spend a lot of time thinking about things and very little time experiencing the world through our bodies, hearts, and souls. This one-dimensional way of experiencing life cuts us off from our feminine power and wisdom. It creates anxious versions of ourselves as well as a self-reinforcing worldview that our thoughts are our entire truth.

There is a better way but it requires awareness, openness, and curiosity—things that don't come naturally to most of us. Our bodies, our emotions, and our intuition all give us valuable information that pours forth from our own inner-wisdom. These sources of understanding and knowledge are generally far more rooted in truth than our thoughts, which are typically based in judgment and fear. When we start believing ourselves more than our thoughts, we find peace.

The Four-Way Stop is a tool I developed as a way to check in with all parts of myself simply and directly—any time, anywhere. It brings me back to the present and allows me to get clear on what I'm feeling, thinking, and experiencing in the moment. It takes me out of my head and back into myself, recalibrates me, and allows me to move forward in my day with intention and integrity.

Once you practice it enough, The Four-Way Stop will become second nature to you. It can be done no matter what's going on around you. Whether you're driving, washing the dishes, speaking on a conference call, putting your kids to bed, or getting your teeth cleaned at the dentist, the Four-Way Stop is a tool that requires nothing more than the privacy of your own mind and a willingness to pause and be present with what the current moment holds for you.

Here's a way to start experimenting with the Four Way Stop:

1. Set an alarm on your phone to go off every hour for the next 12 hours after you wake up (within reasonable parameters of work, school, etc).
2. When the alarm goes off, stop what you're doing and take a few slow inhales and exhales to center yourself.
3. Consciously bring yourself into the present moment.
4. As you begin to turn your awareness inward do the following for as long as feels good.

5. Slowly bring your awareness to your body. Notice without judgment any sensations it may be having. Is it tired? Excited? Sore? Warm? Cold? Tense?

6. Next, turn your awareness to your mind. Notice any thoughts without judgment or agenda. What thoughts are you having that you might not have been aware of until this moment? Are the thoughts positive or negative? Do the thoughts give you energy or drain you? Do they come from a place of creativity, inspiration, or love, or do they come from a place of hate, pain, or fear?

7. Now turn your attention and awareness to your heart. How are you feeling emotionally in the present moment? Are you feeling sad? Frustrated? Stuck? Bored? Restless? Content? Excited? Playful? Do the feelings you're having have any connection to the thoughts you noticed just a moment ago? If so, how?

8. Finally, turn your attention to your soul. By this, I mean become aware of your higher self or inner-wisdom. Are you feeling disconnected from the Divine within you? Cut off? Not in alignment with your sacred self? Or do you feel whole, peaceful, connected, sovereign? Is your intuition trying to tell you something you've been unable to hear before now?

Finish out this two minute exercise with a few additional deep breaths and an intention for your experience of the next hour. At the end of the day, journal on your experience. What did this exercise do for your awareness of what previously went unnoticed in the course of your day-to-day life? What connections did you notice between the experiences of your body, mind, emotions, and soul throughout the day? Was the experience of one directly related to the experience of the others? How can you apply your observations to your broader practice in intentional mindfulness and conscious renewal?

The Four-Way Stop is a way to pause and move from doing to being. It allows us to remember who we are and to be both all that is and nothing more than that in the moment. When we stop what we're doing and allow ourselves to be, we become aware: of our wholeness, our perfection, our completeness. This awareness naturally brings with it the gift of peace because it allows our experience to become real, more full, and more true.

Using Mindfulness to Enhance a Pleasurable Experience

As I mentioned earlier, one way mindfulness can benefit us is through its ability to invite us more deeply into a moment that is already joyful.[44]

Which sounds more like a richly embodied, fully present experience to you:

We were on a long weekend trip to a resort in the Pocono Mountains. I enjoyed myself while playing with my daughters and husband. It was so beautiful. I took some pictures plus a short video and posted the best ones on my Facebook page. It got likes right away. The kids were complaining a lot and between that and the pile of work I knew I had waiting for me back at the office, it was not all that relaxing, but it was nice, I guess. The water was cold plus it had a lot of gross algae

---

[44] An article on the science behind how mindfulness and positive affect effect each other in an upward spiral: Gotink RA, KS Hermans, N. Geschwind, R. De Nooij , W. De Groot, A. E. Speckens. 2016. Mindfulness and mood stimulate each other in an upward spiral: a mindful walking intervention using experience sampling. *Mindfulness (N Y)*. 7(5):1114-1122.

and plant stuff in it, so I didn't want to go in. I sat on the beach with my younger daughter but I quickly got sand in my bathing suit and I noticed that there was a whole area of my leg that I missed shaving.

— or—

We were on a long weekend trip to a resort in the Pocono Mountains. The end of the school year was packed with events and activities and I was reveling in the simple act of stillness in the clean mountain air. I sat in a bathing suit with my hair in a wet bun on the warm shore of the lake, sand crunching between my toes. Surrounding me were thousands of evergreen trees. Their vibrant hues contrasted magically with the deep blue of the sky above. My younger daughter was wearing a purple bathing suit and sitting next to me building a sandcastle. Her terry cloth sun hat shaded her blue eyes and she looked up and smiled at me.

I watched my husband and older daughter in red life vests swimming out to the middle of the lake. They waved and smiled in the late afternoon sun and I felt the delicious warmth in my heart enhanced by the delicious warmth on my shoulders. Gratitude made its still but powerful presence known and I let it wash over me.

Our lives are made up of these moments and both of these accounts of a day in the Poconos are "true." The external circumstances didn't change at all—only the mindset. The feelings such as gratitude, appreciation, and even relief that we seek are available to us all the time. Mindfulness opens up our hearts and allows us to be fully in joyous receipt of all the good flowing to us in the current moment.

Mindfulness enables us to be in the beauty of the present as we let go of controlling, judging, categorizing, ranking, manipulating, planning or analyzing the moment, and instead just let our lives unfold.

Try this:

Every experience can have positive and negative qualities to it. Use mindfulness to turn up the dial on the aspects of the experience that feel good to get the most out of the experience.

- Look at your schedule for the next day. Identify some activities that are going to be taking place that you know you will naturally take some pleasure in, for example, chatting with a coworker during lunch, talking to your mom, taking a long hot shower at the end of the day, or taking your dog for a walk.

- Mentally pre-pave the anticipation of pleasure for yourself by noting what it is about that activity that brings you enjoyment and getting excited for what is to come. Really articulate in your mind what it is you love about that activity. Is it the aroma of the coffee and the warmth of the mug in your hands? Is it the overwhelming energy of love and joy that your dog brings you when you take out his leash? Is it the comfort of your mother's voice after a long day or the feeling of hot water on your skin and the smell of your lavender scented shampoo?

- When you actually start to do the activity, give yourself the gift of full focus. If your mind starts to wander, simply bring it back and note that it wandered without judging it.

- Maintain an attitude of openness and appreciation for the activity by actively choosing thoughts that enhance the experience. For example:

> *I love talking to my mom so much. I love how every time I talk to her I seem to feel comforted and validated. I really appreciate that she takes time out of her day to hear what's going on in my life no matter how busy she is. It's so amazing that even though my mom lives in another state, I can still reach her any time I want to.*

Or...

This shower truly feels incredible! The cold winter weather is tough for me but getting into a hot shower after a long day feels amazing. I love breathing the hot steam into my lungs. I love the pulse of the water on my neck and shoulders. I love having a chance to clear my mind and have a few moments of unadulterated peace. I so appreciate the fact that I have access to this water That's something that's a precious resource to so many in this world but is so readily available to me.

Or...

No matter how many cups of coffee I drink I can't get over how amazing each one tastes. The first sip is the best —it really never gets old. I love feeling the warmth of the mug in my hands. The combination of sweet and bitter on my tongue and the aroma gives me a lovely sensory experience. This is such a fabulous way to start my morning.

You can use this technique with anything you find yourself doing throughout the day. It will give the things you already enjoy deeper meaning and a richer overall experience. Making the choice to do something mindfully is the choice to do it with your whole self. Your life is made up of these moments, and how you live your moments is, of course, how you live your life.

Getting Intimate with Anxiety

It's human to tell ourselves that the way to get rid of pain is to focus on trying to fix it until it's gone. We do this because we believe we can't feel peaceful or happy until we are free from the pain's power over our lives. Yet when we struggle with something or try to force it out of our lives, it tends to give it more power over us. Fighting against pain usually has an effect that is opposite of our goal of more peace because it gives the pain energy and attention that only makes its presence more intense in our experience.

Imagine you're at the bottom of a tall mountain and you want to reach the top. You look at a map and notice that there are several different trails that go up the mountain but they all take meandering, twisty paths through the forest and you want just want to get to the end as quickly as possible. You decide that the best approach is to simply forge your own path and walk straight up the mountain whether there is an official marked trail or not.

A quarter mile up, you come to a patch of poison ivy. You become frustrated and angry that the mountain is getting in the way of your plan. You walk around the poison ivy and return to your intended path as quickly as possible. But as soon as you get back to the trail , you find another issue: there is a stream cutting across your path and it's too deep and wide to jump across safely. You realize you will now have to backtrack to the nearest bridge, which is another quarter mile in the wrong direction and takes you almost back to your starting point.

At this point, you realize that spending your journey mentally fighting against the obstacles on the mountain will probably not get you up the mountain any faster, and it definitely won't make the journey more pleasant. You decide to try it a different way.

You go back to your starting point and change your goal entirely: instead of finding the most efficient path up the mountain, you now want to have the most peaceful experience up the mountain. You decide to start up one of the trails and then go off-trail whenever you see something that is interesting or beautiful to you that you want to see more of. You notice the earthy smell of soil and plants. Your allow your vision to rest on enormous trees and tiny insects. You enjoy the intensity of the light finding its way through the thick branches of the forest.

No longer focused on time, you can now fully immerse yourself in the experience by *responding* with intention to each new twist and turn on your journey instead of *resisting* and *reacting* out of anger or frustration. You still have moments of frustration and aggravation when you take a wrong turn or find yourself at another impasse, but these feelings are no longer the entire story. They exist with space around them to simultaneously experience the good feelings at the same time.

This is what mindfulness is all about: finding a path that navigates in between the pleasant and unpleasant, allows them both to coexist in our experience.

When I was 23 and newly graduated from my Master's degree program, I got my first job as a primary therapist at a psychiatric hospital. I was excited and nervous to start my counseling career, and put a lot of my sense of self into my ability to handle the stress of the job with grace and to excel in my new position.

However, a few weeks into my job I got severely sick. At first I thought it was just a nasty stomach bug, but the symptoms didn't seem to go away no matter what. Day after day, I sat in bed with severe nausea, stomach pains, inability to eat, and an overwhelming sense of panic. Because I didn't know what the problem was, the panic grew with each day I couldn't get to work. I was terrified that I would never be able to figure out what was wrong with me and that I wouldn't be able to return to work in the career that was so precious and important to me and that I had just spent so much time, energy, and money pursuing.

After about a week, I finally tried to force myself to try to go in, but had to pull over to vomit on the way. Feeling defeated, I had to concede that there was no way I could function in a high-stress, fast paced environment, like the one I was trying to get to. More days were spent in bed, barely moving and losing weight and strength by the day.

I eventually saw a specialist who after much speculation and testing diagnosed me with celiac disease: an autoimmune disease that affects the small intestine and causes it to attack itself when gluten is eaten. An endoscopy revealed that my gut had severe damage to it, but I was hugely relieved to have a diagnosis and a clear plan for how to get better. The doctor told me that all I would have to do would be to avoid any food containing gluten for the rest of my life, and my body would heal itself.

I didn't realize that the next six months of healing would continue to be a living hell as my body tried to reverse years of damage. I also didn't realize that one of the symptoms of advanced celiac disease is severe anxiety and panic, due to the damage to the gut where much of the body's serotonin (a neurotransmitter responsible for cognition, mood and anxiety) is manufactured.

I was back at work after my diagnosis, but only because I had no idea if or when I would actually feel better. I didn't think that going on temporary disability wasn't an option because for all I knew, the symptoms might continue for the rest of my life.

At work, we had daily morning rounds where the entire treatment team including other social workers, doctors, nurses, group counselors, and sometimes interns or students would gather in a crowded conference room and each patient's progress and plans for continued treatment or discharge from the hospital would be discussed. The entire process generally took upwards of an hour, and the entire time, I would be having a silent panic attack.

Being in a crowded room of professionals discussing complex mental illness as a new professional myself was anxiety producing enough, but on top of that I had to sit through the meeting feeling like I would either pass out or vomit thanks to the damage in my gut. Of course, the feelings of extreme illness only compounded my anxiety and panic, and in retrospect I can see that the entire situation was a vicious circle: the sicker I felt, the more anxious I felt, and the anxiety would only further trigger more intense physical symptoms, which would take me to a state of complete panic.

So the celiac disease was both a physical cause of my panic attacks and a mental trigger to further compound the anxiety and make the physical symptoms worse. I was making it through work each day, but managing the anxiety in public took every ounce of energy I had, and when I got home, I would collapse into bed and mentally check out with the help of TV or my laptop (smartphones weren't a thing yet).

It wasn't just at work either. Things that might have been a bit draining but still fun in the past like going to a crowded party or going out to eat at a new restaurant now caused me to have a full-blown panic attack. I now understand that with my celiac disease, my brain interpreted the physical symptoms I was experiencing such as nausea, stomach pains and lightheadedness as a trigger to my sympathetic nervous system and reacted with the same level of fear and anxiety as it would with an imminent life-threatening attack. At the time, however, having no idea what was happening or why only made it worse.

When we have a feeling of anxiety that we can't make sense of, our brain scrambles to find the source of the threat so that it can do its job of keeping us safe. For me, I developed a deep aversion to being in crowds of people I didn't know or in unfamiliar situations where I couldn't guarantee that if I started to feel sick or panic that I would have an easy way to escape. The fear that I could either throw up or pass out in public or that I could have an uncontrollable panic attack and would be humiliated in front of colleagues or strangers caused the physical symptoms of my disease to worsen when I was in any scenario where I felt it was possible for that to happen.

In addition to receiving my own counseling at the time to learn new ways of thinking about my physical illness and panic, I also immersed myself in the study of applying mindfulness to my current situation. This is what saved me. While the panic tried to convince me that it had all the power and that I was at its mercy, mindfulness showed me that I could always have peace no matter what the circumstances. While anxiety left me in fear of losing everything that was important to me, mindfulness showed me that the worst thing that could happen to me is an emotion and that there was no emotion I couldn't be present with.

I began to make the connection that mindfulness and thought work were two sides of a coin that together would lead me to a place where I was already healed, already whole, already at peace. In the next section, I'll teach you a three step process that I discovered can be used for any situation we label as painful or negative—including discomfort, worry, anxiety and panic.

Step 1: Move Your Attention Toward the Anxiety

Being present with our anxiety allows us to rid ourselves of the fear of what might happen in the future and the helplessness of how we felt in the past and to accept what is.

Start by moving your attention toward the thing that's causing you fear or pain. I know this sounds counterintuitive—after all, you're trying to reduce the uncomfortable thing's impact on your life, not magnify it by paying more attention to it. But that's the paradox of mindfulness: we stop giving the pain power by running away from it and instead take ownership of our experience. In doing this, we can notice that if we only have *this* moment to get through, the pain of the anxiety is manageable. Luckily, this moment is all we ever have to deal with.

When I was dealing with severe anxiety, I started to notice that if I worried about what would happen in the future, the anxiety would feel unbearable. For example, I would be sitting in a meeting having a silent panic attack but trying to look normal so my coworkers wouldn't notice. If I thought about the fact that if the anxiety got even 1% worse, I might not be able to handle it and I would be embarrassed in front of everyone, then my physical symptoms of upset stomach, lightheadedness and chest pain would suddenly seem to actually get worse. It was as if the physical symptoms sensed my fear and fed on it.

The thoughts would quickly spiral: *"Oh my God, I feel like I'm going to either throw up or pass out right now. That would be so embarassing. Everyone would think I can't handle this job. And what if they're right? What if I'm just not cut out for this? What if I lose the career I worked so hard for? What if I have to live the rest of my life with this crippling anxiety and the anxiety takes away everything important to me? Why is this happening? I'm feeling really lightheaded. I really think I might throw up right on this conference table!"*

Suddenly I felt totally out of control—not just of the current moment, but of my entire life. I felt like everything I worked so hard for was slipping away right there in that conference room, and not surprisingly, that feeling didn't exactly help to lessen the pain of my anxiety or make it more manageable.

Other times, however, I was able to keep myself in the moment and remind myself that although the current experience wasn't pleasant, I was still in control and none of my worst fears were actually happening in *this* moment. Doing this allowed me to be able to stay on top of the anxiety. If all I had to get through was the current moment, and not my entire life, things started to feel a whole lot more manageable.

During the time that I was dealing with the worst of the anxiety, I happened to read an article in one of my professional psychotherapy journals that suggested a technique where if a client felt stuck, the therapist would ask the client if they could speak to the part of them that wasn't stuck. Doing this would help the client separate their larger sense of self from the stuck sense of self, and therefore loosen the hold that the stuck identity had and allow them to move forward.

I tried this with my anxiety and noticed that it did seem to significantly help. Suddenly I wasn't a helpless victim who had lost all control over her life. Instead, I was a person who could observe the anxiety without it becoming my entire identity. I began to understand that even while having severe anxiety, I could also have peace.

Now if I was sitting in a meeting and feeling my anxiety starting to rise, I would choose not to focus on the thought that if it got worse, I might totally lose it and humiliate myself. I would instead start a dialogue in my head where I would speak to the part of myself that wasn't anxious. That part would immediately begin talking and would say things like, *"Yes you're anxious right now, but you've been anxious in front of coworkers many other times, and you've never once done anything to embarrass yourself,"* and *"In this moment, you're handling it just fine. It may not feel great, but that doesn't mean it's bigger or stronger than you are,"* and *"You can always leave this room if you need to. You're not trapped here. People will just think you're going to the bathroom or taking a phone call. You're not stuck. You can get out of this any time it feels like it's too much."*

Maintaining contact with the present moment allowed me to get to a place where I was much more capable of accessing the part of me that was always peaceful no matter what the circumstance. That peaceful part of me might not have been able to stop the pain of the anxiety entirely, but it did allow me to recognize that the anxiety and I were not the same. We were separate. While the anxiety might have been intense, as I connected with the loving, non-judgmental, peaceful part of me, I was no longer a helpless victim to it.

There is always space for peace in the present moment, and luckily that's all life is anyway: one present moment after another (or perhaps

194

one big present moment, but that's a subject for another book). Either way, the suffering of the past and the pain of the future don't exist anywhere but in our own minds. For me, realizing this was a relief of epic proportions. If you're in pain, I hope it will be for you too.

Step 2: Turn Toward the Positive Aspects of the Experience

Looking for the positive aspects of an experience when you're in pain or feel like you're suffering may seem like deluding yourself or just distracting yourself, but it's not. Looking for the positive aspects of an experience is actually about becoming fully aware of the truth of what already exists but you are unable to see. The sun doesn't not exist just because we turn our backs to it. It's always there whether we acknowledge it or not. Likewise, turning ourselves to face the sun isn't distraction or denying our truth. It's opening ourselves up to the deeper reality that was there the whole time.

It's the same for anxiety. Focusing on what's going wrong in our lives or being terrified of what might happen or perseverating about the past doesn't keep us safely grounded in reality, though the anxiety might try to convince us otherwise. Just the opposite—focusing on the painful parts of life blinds us to the beautiful parts that are right there all along too.

As I tell my clients, it's okay to pitch a tent in anxiety, but don't build your home there. Meaning, it's okay to be present with and acknowledge that things are not the way you would like them to be, but don't allow yourself to fall into the false belief that your pain is the entire story, because it never is. Your pain or anxiety may be an aspect of your experience, but it's never your entire identity unless you choose it to be.

When we are in a state of anxiety, our minds tend to view our lives through that lens but the truth is that life is never black and white; it's always much more nuanced. Who would you be if you didn't have the identity of a person who is defined by the things that are causing you pain in your life? To find out, you would have to allow space for the experience to not be all bad.

Events are never all bad or all good, though our minds like to categorize them as such. Looking back on my life, it's clear that the lowest, most difficult most challenging moments all contained within them aspects of beauty and peace. For example, when I was dealing with the most severe anxiety, I started to feel like my life was a living hell. I began and ended the day with panic, and was basically living life on a continuum between "very anxious" and "literally about to pass out from the level of anxiety I'm experiencing right now."

Despite that, I can also look back and, with no effort at all, recall the many beautiful moments that came out of the experience: the support of my friends and family when I was finally able to open up to them about what I was going through, letting go of lifelong stories about the need to be accepted by everyone, and learning that peace was always available to me.

There were also peaceful walks through the fall leaves, quiet afternoons with a good book, good times with friends, and growing in my profession. These moments were moments of pure love and connection. These moments were heightened in their beauty and pleasure because they were contrasted with the hard parts.

As I mentioned earlier, mindfulness is a state of awareness, openness, and focus. In the years since I went through the experience of my diagnosis and slow recovery from celiac disease, I've endeavored to practice it in everything I do—especially when it's hard, and all I want to do is zone out, numb, or close myself off. Of course, I do this extremely imperfectly, but that's okay—perfection was never the goal—presence and peace always were.

In fact, I've come to think of mindfulness and peace as being synonymous. They both carry with them the quality of freedom: to always begin again, to never be defined by our circumstances, and to always have access to the feelings of wisdom, beauty, joy, and connection in every moment.

Step 3: Remember Your Free Will

Mindfulness is not about not caring or being oblivious to the truth of our situation. It is, however, about moving away from fight-or-flight mode where we are easily swayed to act in ways don't honor ourselves and that have a net effect of causing us more suffering. In other words, mindfulness reminds us of our choice to respond instead of react. That choice is our free will, and that choice is our way to peace.[45]

In my work with women over the past twelve years, I have found that one of the greatest impediments to their peace is the feeling that they are out of control in their lives—that something bad is happening to them and there's nothing they can do about it. In order to remember our free will in a situation, we must first stop judging that situation. Judging destroys our ability to be objective and locks us into automatic responses that don't serve us.

---

[45] A philosophical and practical look at the way mindfulness cultivates awareness over mental states that undermine our freedom and free will: Repetti, R. 2010. Meditation and mental freedom: A Buddhist theory of free will. *Journal of Buddhist Ethics*. 17: 166-212.

When I was in the height of physical illness and anxiety from my celiac disease diagnosis, I was also in the height of feeling powerless. I believed my judgments and fears about the situation to be the truth and therefore of course felt like a victim to them. Looking back, I can now see that had I known to take a step back and become an impartial observer of both my thoughts and the situation, I would have been able to find a lot more peace.[46]

It's important to note that when we find our minds judging, we don't have to judge ourselves about the judging or try to make ourselves stop. We only need to notice that judging is what's happening and to let that observation come fully into our awareness without trying to fix it. When we become the observer, we also become the one with the power to consciously let go.

All this doesn't mean that we should be passive or resigned to reality or try to trick ourselves into not believing in it. After all, Steps 1 and 2 were entirely about being fully present with reality. That being said, our recognition of our free will happens when we allow ourselves to accept what is. That doesn't mean we don't care or don't take action. It

---

[46] My experience is in line with this research: Hayes, S. C., R. Bissett, Z. Korn, R. D. Zettle, I. Rosenfarb, L. Cooper, et al. 1999. The impact of acceptance versus control rationales on pain tolerance. *The Psychological Record.* 49:33-47.

doesn't mean we don't have painful feelings about it. All those things can still happen—they just now happen with consciousness.

For example, I recently planned a get-together with four friends and their families at my house. These friends all have a lot going on in their lives with careers and kids and living life, so I planned the get-together two months in advance to make sure everyone would be able to make it. On the day of, however, two of the friends informed me that they would not be able to make it. Their reasons for not coming were completely reasonable and valid, and yet I felt annoyed and angry.

It was hard not to judge those feelings because as I said, my friends' reasons for canceling last minute were totally understandable, but I allowed myself to be with those feelings anyway as I went through my day making preparations for the party. Being with those feelings allowed me to move through them and to get to the deeper feelings of disappointment and sadness that were below the surface.

As I allowed myself to be with my feelings, without effort, my focus started to shift to the friends who were still coming and the fun, laid-back evening my family and I were about to have. Had I tried to impose judgments about what I should be thinking or feeling in that situation, or how things or people should be different, I would have gone into a negative thought spiral and effectively ruined my own evening.

Free will came in my choice to be with what was—both in my mind and in the situation itself. This choice allowed me to recognize that my true power lay not in my ability to change things or even change my feelings about them, but in my ability to be with it all wholeheartedly. By being with it all, I was paradoxically able to let go. And in letting go, I found peace.

The Art of Conscious Living Through Meditation

If you stop and pay attention to what's going on in your mind at any given moment, you'll notice a ton of chatter going on. For example, right now I'm typing this in my basement home office and my husband is upstairs watching a movie while the kids are at my mom's for a visit. I would like to think I'm completely focused on what I'm writing, but the truth is, my thoughts are constantly going off in their own direction:

That movie is loud. Sounds like he's watching The Shining. Why does he always listen to movies so loudly? I hope he's not losing his hearing like his grandfather. Maybe I should ask him to turn it down. But it's almost over, so it's fine. I can concentrate...let's see, what am I trying to write here...So, thinking about thoughts—what else do I want to say in this part? Is that rain I hear outside? I can't believe it's still raining. It's been raining since yesterday! I guess it's a good thing it's not snow. But is the rain a sign of global warming? I hope it doesn't all freeze tomorrow. I can't deal with another 2 hour delay! Okay, back to the writing. Thinking about thinking... How much time do I have left to work on this? It's 1:25 now. What time were we supposed to pick up the kids? My feet are cold but I really don't feel like going upstairs to get socks right now. I'll just put some pillows on top of them. There. That's kind of better. I just can't move my feet or the pillows will fall off...

And so it goes, on and on and on. Our mind is always intruding on our experience with at best banal narration of what's going on and at worst harsh judgment and criticism.

If we consistently tell ourselves the same story and that story is a negative one, we eventually stop questioning the truth of the story and start living as if it were fact. Our unquestioning acceptance of our negative thoughts as truth also leads us to sacrifice present moment happiness and peace in service of our far off goals. We believe that when we achieve that next big promotion or make X more money or finally find a partner we will be happy. But when we get there, our level of happiness remains the same as its always been.

In addition to living in the future, our thoughts also lead us to relive past moments over and over again, perseverating about what we did wrong or how angry we are because of someone else's actions or how much better our lives would be if something that already happened had gone differently. They steal the present moment from us, causing us to miss how peaceful, perfect, and easy things are in THIS moment.

Meditation is one of the fastest and simplest ways to renew yourself because it trains your mind to return to the present moment quickly, constantly and consistently—even and especially when you're feeling stressed, overwhelmed or stuck. It is a tool to access our higher self and connect with our inner-wisdom. It trains our busy minds to slow down and be in the moment where the tensions, stresses, and pain of our lives are no longer adversaries but friends and partners in our healing.[47]

Meditation helps give us confidence in our ability to effectively deal with the challenges of our lives. It gives us a greater sense of control and freedom in life, and ultimately helps us cultivate a greater sense of meaning in who we are and how we live.

When we meditate, we free ourselves from the shackles of our busy minds, including negative self-talk and become able to look at the

---

[47] An article that summarizes some of the many studies that have been done on the benefits of meditation including reduction in stress, anxiety, and depression, reduction in physical and psychological pain, improved memory, and a myriad of positive physical effects: Sharma, H. 2015. Meditation: Process and effects. *Ayu*. Sharma H. Meditation: Process and effects. *Ayu*. 2015;36(3):233-7.

world from a place of stillness and knowing. We realize that thinking something doesn't make it true, and that living in the margin between conscious thought and action gives allows us to act with integrity.

Many women I work with have tried and given up on meditation because they feel it's too hard or it doesn't work for them. Unfortunately, they are usually misinformed about the purpose of meditation, believing it to be to clear their minds entirely of thoughts for the duration of the session. Being unable to do this for longer than a few seconds, they become discouraged and give up.

In truth, the goal of meditation is not to stop your thoughts entirely, but simply to become aware of them. We do this by noticing without judgment that we're having thoughts and then returning to the anchor of our breath over and over again. If your mind wanders ninety-nine times during a meditation session, but you re-anchor your breath a hundred times, you've had a "successful" meditation session because you've created new neural pathways in your brain that will allow it to work with increased clarity, focus, and intention all the time.[48]

---

[48] More on this in the book: Kabat-Zinn, J. 2018. *Meditation is Not What You Think*. New York: Hachette.

I've had more clients than I can count tell me that they don't feel that they have time in their day to devote to meditating because their lives and schedules are jam-packed with work, kids, household responsibilities, and family obligations. When I suggest that carving out ten minutes to consistently meditate can exponentially increase their feelings of peace, ease, and intention in their lives, they will double down in trying to explain to me that it sounds like a good idea but they jump out of bed in the morning already feeling behind and exhausted for the day and don't get a moment to rest again until their head hits the pillow at night.

They would love to take a few minutes for themselves, they tell me, but it's really not possible. Like many of us, these women are so attached to stories that equates busyness with worthiness that they believe they're powerless over the chaos and stress that fill their lives. They have to work and take care of their families and manage their lives and all that, they tell themselves simply doesn't allow for a single ten minute chunk of time where the only "goal" is consciousness.

I ask my clients what kind of life they're living if they literally can't get off the treadmill of obligation and action for ten minutes during a 1,440 minute day. I then explain that when you have a belief that you're too busy to take proper care of yourself, you create in your life a vicious cycle in which you operate with increasingly less resources. This leads to the unfortunate outcome where the life you worked so hard for and the life you actually want to live become two very different things and it's why most of my clients come to therapy in the first place.

To live with integrity means to embrace that you are whole, perfect, and complete exactly as you are right now. This truth is impossible to experience when you're constantly in that state of overwhelm, exhaustion, and resentment. Peace is about living a life of dignity and self-respect and a life where you feel frazzled and crazed all the time is not conducive to that.

Making Yourself a Non-Negotiable

Taking time to center yourself at least once in your day not only has the positive benefits of rewiring your brain to better manage stress, pain, anxiety, boredom, and other forms of mental suffering, it also on a larger level reinforces the belief that you're worth being taken care of. Making yourself a non-negotiable allows for the conscious feeling of self-love and the simple joy of ten minutes of peaceful, judgment-free existence.

The purpose of meditation isn't to relax, although deep states of relaxation can accompany meditation practice. The purpose of meditation is to find peace and release suffering no matter what the present moment is bringing to us. It is a path to develop new inner-wisdom and a new sense of control based on what is actually in our control: our capacity for acceptance and presence. When we meditate, we are not telling ourselves that only certain feelings or circumstances are tolerable. We see all feelings and situations as valid and worthy of being accepted, noticed, and deeply experienced.

Throughout your life, there have likely been parts of yourself (maybe it even feels like the majority of parts) that you desperately wish you could change. "If this thing were different, you think, my life would be so much better. I would be happier, finally at peace. My life would finally be good." Maybe it's your weight. Maybe it's anxiety. Maybe it's a deep feeling of resentment toward someone who hurt you long ago. The specifics aren't all that important because feelings are universal. Whatever it is, there is likely suffering there with it.

Meditation is a conduit through which we can experience the presence of all that is loving and peaceful and sacred in the present moment— no matter what our external experience or internal thoughts are. Having a complete experience of love and peace is what we have always wanted but perhaps never received from those from whom we need it most: our parents, our siblings, our friends, our enemies, our spouses, our kids, strangers, etc. But we can't ask others to give us more than we are able to give ourselves. How can we expect unconditional love and approval from the world when we find it impossible to give it to ourselves?

Let's stop trying to make ourselves something different than we already are—to be more "good," "nice," "happy," "motivated," "organized," or whatever we think we need to be before we can finally be worthy. Instead, let's turn in to the basic experience of being who we really are and accepting peace in whatever we find.

Try this exercise and notice what comes up:

- Set a timer for ten or fifteen minutes.
- Lie on your back or sit upright—whichever feels more comfortable. If you are sitting, keep your spine upright (imagine a string pulling you up from the top of your head) and let your shoulders relax.
- Gently close your eyes.
- Bring your focus to your breath, and allow your belly to rise with each inward breath and fall with each outward breath.
- Keep your attention on each inward breath as it goes in and each outward breath as it goes out.
- Every time you notice your attention has wandered, take note of where it has gone and then turn your attention back to your breath.
- Do not put judgments on your time with your breath or decide that you're "not doing it right." Do not enter into this time with a goal like "I need to get relaxed" or "I need to clear my mind." Instead of doing, just focus on being. Meditation has no goal but for you to be yourself. And you already are.

Shifting Into Being

Mariana came to me because she was experiencing panic attacks at work and before bed. She had just ended a long-term relationship with a woman who turned out to have been unfaithful most of the time they were together. While not an alcoholic, Mariana was regularly overdoing it with alcohol and food to soothe her nerves after another anxiety ridden, stressful day. She felt stuck and was racked with shame for not feeling better, doing better, or acting better in pretty much all areas of her life.

Mariana took responsibility for her ex-girlfriend's behavior, believing that if she had done things differently, or gotten her girlfriend the help she needed when she needed it, things would be different. Mariana also expressed a desire to stop using food and wine to buffer away her difficult feelings but found herself in such a low place after a hard day at work, that she didn't feel she had any other way to cope.

Our counseling sessions focused on targeting some of the negative self-talk that Mariana engaged in on a near-constant basis. Together we looked at whether the shame-inducing stories that she was telling herself were accurate or just long-held fixed beliefs that she had never bothered to question. As Mariana began to challenge many of her negative beliefs about herself, she also began to understand and loosen her grip on her perfectionistic and codependent tendencies.

To start managing her overactive nervous system, I suggested Mariana meditate for five to fifteen minutes, twice per day, using an app such as Calm or HeadSpace to help her get started. I thought this would be particularly helpful before bed when anxiety tended to be high, and asked her to report back to me her findings over the next few weeks.

In our next sessions, Mariana appeared visibly more relaxed with less tension in her face and body, and more strength and clarity in her voice. She told me that she tried meditating when she got home from our session the previous week and had absolutely loved it. For the first time in her life, she had given herself permission to quiet the constantly critical voice in her head and just be present with nothing to fix, achieve, or do. In fact, Mariana loved it so much, she was carving out time as soon as she woke up and as soon as she got home from work to turn on a meditation app or some music and sit in silence.

By the second month of meditating regularly, Mariana had gone several weeks without a panic attack and was feeling much more centered and able to get through the day without feeling like she was struggling every moment. She still had frequent negative thoughts about herself, but meditating was beginning to give her the ability to pause and question the thoughts instead of automatically believing them.

Over time, Mariana was more and more able to challenge her feelings of shame, eventually coming to the conclusion that she was not responsible for her ex's behavior and that she deserved to be in a relationship where she felt loved and cared for. Her reliance on food and alcohol to avoid negative feelings slowly dropped off as she learned to instead sit with them. She now knew there was no feeling she couldn't handle and that if she allowed herself to feel them fully, they would eventually dissipate on their own. The less she feared uncomfortable feelings, the less they seemed to come up.

Slowly, Mariana began to let go of other toxic relationships in her life and to surround herself with positive people who reinforced her sense of value and self-worth. The negative self-talk still happened, but with far less frequency and intensity, and with far less impact on her daily functioning. Although meditation wasn't the answer to all of Mariana's problems, it was a crucial tool in calming her hypersensitive nervous system, giving her mental space and peace of mind and allowing her to build a life with integrity to who she really was at her core. Meditation is renewal for our minds, bodies, and souls. It makes us new again in the most fundamental of ways. Like Mariana, I encourage you to approach meditation with a curious mind. Your inner-perfectionist might get loud, questioning whether you're doing it right, telling you it's hard or boring or that you're just not good at it.

That's okay. Meditation is all about embracing the "and" in life. You can be bored or anxious or fearful **and** still experience benefit of greater peace. Your mind can wander the entire ten minutes **and** as long as you bring it back to your breath when you notice, you are benefitting. The same worries and stresses will still be there when your session is over **and** you'll find that you are able to approach them from a more peaceful, connected place.

Peace at Last

It can be an ironic relief to know that the greatest block to peace is ourselves. It means that the most direct path to peace is also through us. We don't have to wait for people or circumstances to change—peace is available to us in every moment.

Chasing outside approval compromises our relationships with ourselves, our loved ones, and our innermost being. It's time to leave behind the weight of competition, people-pleasing and exhaustion and instead craft a life founded in love and created with intention and integrity.

The more we hustle for love, approval, and recognition, the more disconnected we become from the very things we desire most. Maybe it's possible to have all the things we want: connection to others and ourselves, the opportunity for peace in every moment regardless of the circumstances, and the experience of unconditional love. We just can't get to those things by chasing what we once thought would get us there: the appearance perfection, external accolades, and being someone other than who we really are.

We can easily lose ourselves as we hustle, in search of an identity that we think will make us finally good or worthy of love in the eyes of others. In this pursuit, we wind up feeling used and resentful. Our lives become focused on the places where there's not enough time, energy, money, or love and we lose our capacity to experience the sacredness of the moment. We are raised to believe that more is always more and that there is always more to be and do in every aspect of life. The notion of intentionally keeping things small and simple is not something that generally occurs to us or makes a whole lot of sense at first glance.

Most of us grow up to become deeply invested in what others believe about us. We want them to see us as "good," which usually translates to hardworking, capable, and having it all together. We believe that our ideal selves live somewhere in an imaginary future that we can only get to through suffering and sacrifice. We also believe that suffering and sacrifice are non-negotiables for having happiness, safety, and security.

No wonder we lose sight of peace in our lives. No wonder we lose ourselves. The journey started with the premise that we're not good enough, and, full circle, it will always end there too.

We can't chase peace outside ourselves and miraculously find it within. We can't wait for external circumstances to perfectly align to give us peace. We have to claim it for ourselves, moment by moment.

A mindset that you're failing to measure up to your potential feels very different from being honest with yourself about what you're capable of doing without losing yourself in the process. When we own who we are (and are not), we find freedom. We find peace. We find ourselves.

We have all had the experience in our lives of feeling like we've become someone we didn't want to be—someone we didn't particularly like—in order to survive. Maybe for you that time is now. Maybe you've convinced yourself that dignity and integrity aren't luxuries you've been able to afford yourself for one reason or another. To exercise your own free will over your life may feel like an impossible dream.

The bottom line is you can choose a path of knowing and honoring yourself or you can choose a path of forceful, unceremonious action in a direction you believe you "should" be going. You can't be in two places at once, and so ultimately a decision must be made about which path you are going to spend the rest of your life traveling.

Before I chose the journey of peace, my beliefs included:

- Doing things that rob me of my peace sucks, but it's necessary if I ever want to be happy.
- Hustling for everything good in my life will make me loved.

- Doing what I'm "supposed" to do will keep me safe.
- Doing things that don't make me happy is necessary to have value as a woman.

In the course of my own journey, I have come to realize that doing things that aren't in alignment with my highest self leads to fear upon fear, anxiety, comparison, jealousy, confusion, resentment, lack of satisfaction with what I have in the moment, and being a person I don't like to be. I have discovered that what I want most in life are the very things only I can give to myself: presence, wholeheartedness, creativity, peace, and connection. I have learned that despite the current dogma that limitations are something to be overcome, in my life, limitations are also something to embraced and honored.

For much of my life, I have been searching for people and situations that will make me feel taken care of and supported. By honoring who I am physically, emotionally, and spiritually, I have found those feelings to be always accessible to me, through me. And much to my surprise, I have found that suffering is not a prerequisite to being cared for, supported, valued, loved, safe, happy, creative or peaceful.

Suffering is not a sign that we need to dig our heels in deeper, try harder, hold out or give in. In fact, finding the edges of our limitations and accessing peace need never involve suffering. Suffering, I have discovered, is a sign that I'm *not* on the right path—that I'm not on *my* path.

I have slowly but surely learned the difference between challenging myself and sacrificing myself. One makes me more of who I am. The other makes me less. One leaves me empty, the other leaves me full: of the right things in the right quantities.

Here is what the peaceful way has blessed me with:

- A life that feels right-sized for my strengths and limitations— one where I have more than enough time and energy each day to care for myself, have fun, be creative, and spending loving, quality time with the people I love (including myself).
- The ability to do deeper work and have a far greater positive impact on women than I would if I were trying to help others while navigating a chaotic personal life.
- Fun and play, gentleness and rest, ease and abundance in significant, consistent quantities.
- Letting myself be seen and loved for who I am, not what I achieve or sacrifice.
- The belief and the experience that nothing is too good to be true.

- A deeply-held respect for myself and my humanness and my divinity.

- Honoring my truth, which is the truth of love's presence in all things.

- Clarity, intention, integrity, sovereignty.

- The feeling that I am both loved and loving, seeing and seen; that I matter and that things can matter to me without sacrificing my peace.

The way of the peaceful woman is the way of freedom: freedom from resistance to who you are and what your life is and freedom to love whatever the present moment brings you. Before we spend any more time trying to force change on ourselves or other people in the pursuit of feeling better, let's first get to know ourselves, to be deeply intimate and present with ourselves, and to love who we are and what we're experiencing without judgment or a desire to fix or make it different/better.

If there is one thing I hope you take with you as you leave this book, it's this: before you do anything, ask yourself, *does this honor me?* If the answer is no, then you can be sure it is not the peaceful way for you.

I honor *you* for taking this journey with me.

Closing Thoughts

As the journey of reading this book and doing its exercises comes to an end, and the journey of the rest of your life continues on, reflect on these questions in your journal to integrate what you have learned about yourself and your own peaceful path.

- Where in your life has mind*less*ness become the dominant mode of operating?

- Where have you been able to integrate mindfulness and how did it change your experience?

- What is your typical way of "buffering" unpleasant or uncomfortable feelings (i.e. screens, food, drinking, gossip)?

- Did you try the mindful eating exercise in this section? How did it change your experience of eating? What blocks do you anticipate would make it difficult to continue this practice on a daily basis? If you haven't tried it, what got in the way?

- How can you use mindfulness to enhance everyday activities? What net impact do you think this would have on how you experience your life in general?

- Have you struggled with anxiety or other painful feelings? What have you done to avoid those feelings in the past? What do you think would happen if you instead allowed them to be present?

- What is your greatest fear? Why? How does this fear affect how you live your life? What would your life look like if you didn't have this fear?

- Think back to a recent painful experience. Looking back, were there any opportunities that were missed for peace to coexist with the pain?

- What is the relationship between control and peace for you? Does the pursuit of control over your life or over others enhance or serve as an impediment to peace for you?

- Did you try the meditation exercise? What thoughts, feelings, or experiences came up for you?

- Is meditation something that you would like to incorporate into your daily life? What would the benefits be? What might make a commitment to a daily meditation practice challenging?

- Has your definition of peace changed in reading this book? If so, how?

- What is your intention for integrating what you have learned about yourself into your life?

About the Author

Amy Beth Acker, LCSW is a psychotherapist in private practice in Somerville, NJ where she works with women individually and in groups. She received her master's degree from NYU and she holds additional certificates in trauma, mindfulness, and clinical supervision of provisionally licensed clinicians.

Amy is an expert in women's issues and specializes in working with hard-working women who struggle with anxiety, perfectionism, or people-pleasing.

For more of Amy's writing or to connect, please visit AmyBethAcker.com.

Acknowledgements

My deepest appreciation to my clients who never cease to astound me with their strength, inner-wisdom, and integrity. I am honored and humbled to have entered your lives.

Chris: for everything. You are everything, but most of all love.

Violet and Emily: for being my greatest teachers and greatest inspiration. There are no words for my love for you.

Ellen Sterman, Arnold Sterman, Kelly Baldinger, and Xialou Jaing-Jhonsa: for your invaluable feedback and editing services.

Hannah Ratzlaff: for knowing me from the start and for your never-ending support.

Florence Muson: for knowing I was a writer before I did.

My friends and family: for your belief in my writing, and encouragement and for always being there.

To God: for giving me the words, the courage, the understanding that love is all there is.

An Invitation

For more of my writing and free resources, tips, and tools to help you awaken the power of you, create a life you love, and set yourself free, I invite you to join me at **amybethacker.com.** To claim your free bonus ebook, *Peaceful Body*, please visit amybethacker.com/bonus.

Please Leave a Review

Thank you for reading this book. I hope you enjoyed it, and are well on your way to finding more peace in your life.

Now I'd like to ask you for a small favor. Would you kindly take a moment to leave an honest review on Amazon?

It would mean the world to me, and I honor and appreciate the time you take to write it!

Warmly,

Amy

Made in the USA
Middletown, DE
05 March 2020